Rosa Parks

In Her Own Words

Rosa Parks
In Her Own Words

Susan Reyburn   WITH A FOREWORD BY CARLA D. HAYDEN, LIBRARIAN OF CONGRESS

THE UNIVERSITY OF GEORGIA PRESS   ATHENS
IN ASSOCIATION WITH THE LIBRARY OF CONGRESS

*A Sarah Mills Hodge
Fund Publication*

This publication is made
possible, in part, through
a grant from the Hodge
Foundation in memory of its
founder, Sarah Mills Hodge,
who devoted her life to the
relief and education of African
Americans in Savannah,
Georgia.

Published by the University of Georgia Press
Athens, Georgia 30602
www.ugapress.org
in association with the Library of Congress

© 2020 by The Library of Congress
All rights reserved
Designed by Erin Kirk New
Set in Miller Text
Printed and bound by Versa Press
The paper in this book meets the guidelines for
permanence and durability of the Committee on
Production Guidelines for Book Longevity of the
Council on Library Resources.

Most University of Georgia Press titles are
available from popular e-book vendors.

Printed in the United States of America
23 22 21 20 19 P 5 4 3 2 1

Library of Congress Control Number: 2019947019
ISBN: 9780820356921 (pbk: alk. paper)
ISBN: 9780820357218 (ebook)

Contents

So much to remember

Rosa Parks, ca. 1956

Foreword

In her book *Quiet Strength*, Rosa Parks reflected on a dozen topics, from fear to the future, and how she dealt with each during a long and eventful life. The differences between what is contained in that book of accumulated wisdom and her earlier writings detailing a toilsome childhood, the strain of sudden celebrity, and the often perilous and demanding nature of her work are stark and significant. The Rosa Parks we meet here in her manuscripts is not always writing for publication or posterity; she is often writing in the moment or for herself.

Parks's powerful story and her long fight for justice have always resonated with me, and as the first woman and African American to serve as the Librarian of Congress, I take special pleasure in having the Rosa Parks Collection housed here at the nation's library. The collection arrived in 2014, and through the generosity of the Howard G. Buffet Foundation, the papers were made a permanent gift two years later. The collection comprises some ten thousand items drawn from both Parks's private life and her decades of work for civil rights. Items include family photos and correspondence, her handwritten recollections and contemplations, and private notes to herself as she endured the Montgomery Bus Boycott and its painful aftermath. Materials from the Highlander Folk School, the NAACP, the Southern Christian Leadership Conference, and the Rosa and Raymond Parks Institute for Self-Development trace her growth from a dedicated civil rights worker to a national figure who was still actively engaged in social causes in her eighties.

With the publication of *Rosa Parks: In Her Own Words*, the Library of Congress is pleased to share a rarely seen view of an extraordinary woman through her private writings and in her own hand. These writings reveal her keen observations, youthful rage, strong faith, and ongoing hope, as well as an abiding love for those closest to her.

I encourage you to visit the Library of Congress in person or online at www.loc.gov to learn more about Rosa Parks and the civil rights movement and their crucial contributions to American society.

Carla D. Hayden
LIBRARIAN OF CONGRESS

Timeline

1909   The National Association for the Advancement of Colored People (NAACP) is founded in New York City.

1913   Rosa Louise McCauley is born on February 4 in Tuskegee, Alabama.

1915   James McCauley (father) abandons the family.
Sylvester McCauley (brother) is born.
President Woodrow Wilson permits racial segregation of employees in federal executive agencies.

1917   The McCauleys move to Pine Level, Alabama.
Congress declares war on Germany and the United States enters World War I.

1918   Begins school.

1924   Moves in with an aunt in Montgomery, Alabama, to attend Miss White's School for Girls.
The Immigration Act of 1924 prohibits immigrants from Asia and sets quotas for others.

1925   The Brotherhood of Sleeping Car Porters union is founded and is active in early efforts to desegregate employment in the South.

1928   Starts high school; later drops out to tend to her sick mother and grandmother.
Does domestic and farm work.

1929   Begins attending high school classes at Alabama State College in Montgomery.
The stock market crashes, spurring the Great Depression.

1931   Meets Raymond Parks. Supports his campaign to free the "Scottsboro Boys," who were falsely accused of rape and sentenced to death.

1932   Marries Raymond Parks on December 18.

1933   Earns high school diploma. Earns living as a seamstress and office worker.

1941   Begins working at Maxwell Field, an integrated U.S. military base.
The United States enters World War II. Black men and women serve in segregated military units.

1942   The Congress of Racial Equality (CORE) is founded in Chicago.

| 1943 | Attends her first meeting of the NAACP's Montgomery chapter. Attempts to register to vote but is denied. |

| 1944 | Attempts to register to vote but is again denied. |
| | Investigates case of rape victim Recy Taylor and cofounds a justice committee on her behalf. |

| 1945 | Is finally granted a voting certificate. |
| | World War II ends; the United States and the Soviet Union become world superpowers. |

| 1946 | The U.S. Supreme Court bans segregation on interstate bus travel. |

1947	CORE begins Freedom Rides in the upper South to test the desegregation of interstate bus travel; nine Freedom Riders are arrested and jailed.
	Jackie Robinson integrates Major League Baseball.
	President Harry S. Truman's Committee on Civil Rights issues its report, *To Secure These Rights*, which condemns racial injustices.

| 1948 | The Cold War between the West and the Eastern Bloc led by atomic superpowers the United States and the Soviet Union begins. |
| | President Truman orders the desegregation of the military. |

| 1954 | The U.S. Supreme Court rules in *Brown v. Board of Education* that segregated public schools are unconstitutional. White Citizens' Councils form in the South to resist integration. |

1955	Meets Martin Luther King Jr. in Montgomery.
	Attends summer session on school desegregation at Highlander Folk School in Monteagle, Tennessee.
	Emmett Till is murdered in Money, Mississippi. The crime receives national coverage.
	Is arrested for disorderly conduct on a segregated city bus, December 1, and four days later is found guilty of violating local law.
	Montgomery Bus Boycott begins, December 5.

1956	Loses her job as a seamstress at Montgomery Fair department store.
	Is indicted with others for staging the bus boycott.
	Browder v. Gayle, challenging Montgomery's segregated bus law, reaches the U.S. Supreme Court.
	Nineteen U.S. senators and eighty-two House representatives issue the "Southern Manifesto" resisting desegregation.
	After the U.S. Supreme Court affirms that bus segregation is unconstitutional, the 381-day boycott ends.

1957	President Dwight D. Eisenhower signs the Civil Rights Act of 1957, guaranteeing all citizens the right to vote.
	Federal troops protect black students attending Central High School in Little Rock, Arkansas.
	The Southern Christian Leadership Conference is formed in Atlanta.
	Moves with husband and mother to Detroit.
	Begins working at the Hampton Institute in Hampton, Virginia.

1958	Late in the year, leaves the Hampton Institute; returns to Detroit. Works as a seamstress.
1960	The Student Non-violent Coordinating Committee (SNCC) is formed.
1961	Freedom Rides begin in the Deep South.
	President John F. Kennedy signs an executive order forbidding discrimination in hiring federal government employees and introduces affirmative action.
1963	President Kennedy sends federal troops to the University of Alabama, Tuscaloosa, to protect two black students who enroll.
	Attends the March on Washington, where Martin Luther King Jr. delivers his "I Have a Dream" speech.
	Becomes more involved in Detroit community issues.
	The Sixteenth Street Church in Birmingham, Alabama, is bombed, killing four girls.
	NAACP field secretary Medgar Evers is assassinated in Jackson, Mississippi.
	President Kennedy is assassinated.
1964	President Lyndon B. Johnson signs the Civil Rights Act of 1964, which outlaws employment discrimination.
	Freedom Summer, a campaign to register black voters in Mississippi, begins.
	Three civil rights workers are subsequently murdered. Martin Luther King Jr. is awarded the Nobel Peace Prize.
	Works on John Conyers's successful campaign for Congress; he credits her for his victory.
1965	Begins working in the Detroit office of Congressman Conyers.
	Participates in the March from Selma to Montgomery.
	President Johnson signs the Voting Rights Act of 1965, guaranteeing all citizens the right to vote.
1967	A riot breaks out in Detroit, leaving forty-three dead. The Parks family suffers property damage.
	The U.S. Supreme Court rules in *Loving v. Virginia* that state bans on interracial marriage are unconstitutional.
1968	The Kerner Commission issues its report on the recent riots that erupted in major American cities, concluding, "Our nation is moving toward two societies, one black, one white—separate and unequal."
1974	Cofounds the Free Joan Little Defense Committee in Detroit; Little's case is the first in which a woman charged with murder successfully claims self-defense from a sexual assault.
1977	Raymond Parks (husband) dies at seventy-four.
	Sylvester McCauley (brother) dies at sixty-two.

1979   Is awarded the NAACP's Spingarn Medal.
       Leona McCauley (mother) dies at ninety-one.

1980   On the twenty-fifth anniversary of the bus boycott, the *Detroit News* and the
       Detroit Public School system establish the Rosa Parks Scholarship Foundation.

1987   Establishes, with Elaine Steele, the Rosa and Raymond Parks Institute for
       Self Development to assist and instruct youth.

1988   Retires from Congressman Conyers's office.

1991   A bronze bust of her is unveiled at the National Portrait Gallery in
       Washington, D.C.

1992   Publishes her autobiography, *My Story*.

1994   Is robbed and assaulted in her Detroit home.
       Publishes *Quiet Strength*, her book of short reflections.

1995   Addresses the Million Man March in Washington, D.C.

1996   Is awarded the Presidential Medal of Freedom by President Bill Clinton.
       Publishes *Dear Mrs. Parks: A Dialogue with Today's Youth*.

1997   Michigan declares the first Monday after February 4 as Rosa Parks Day.

1999   Receives the Congressional Gold Medal of Honor; attends the State of the
       Union address, Washington, D.C.

2000   The Rosa Parks Museum and Library of Troy State University opens in Montgomery on the
       forty-fifth anniversary of her arrest.

2002   CBS broadcasts the television movie *The Rosa Parks Story*, starring
       Angela Bassett.

2003   Learns she has progressive dementia.

2005   Dies at home in Detroit on October 24; lies in honor at the U.S. Capitol,
       October 30–31.

2013   Her bronze likeness, shown seated, is dedicated in Statuary Hall
       in the U.S. Capitol.

Hurt, harm and danger

The dark closet of my mind

So much to remember

Introduction

On the back of a pharmacy bag, between the lines of a church bulletin, inside a department store pocket calendar, across envelopes, receipts, notepaper, and stationery—whatever was at hand—Rosa Parks wrote. She did so in clear, rightward cursive, as one might expect from a schoolteacher's daughter. A copious notetaker, faithful letter writer, and author of speeches and autobiography, she also penned philosophical nuggets and hopeful contemplations, her prose direct and precise. And in the aftermath of her clash with Jim Crow aboard a city bus in Montgomery, Alabama, Parks documented her childhood encounters with racism and her growing awareness of how segregation affected—and infected—the lives of everyone it touched, black and white.

A middle-aged black woman, Parks still had another half-century—more than half of her lifetime—yet to live after her arrest on December 1, 1955, for refusing to give up her bus seat to a white passenger. The subsequent bus boycott made her a public figure and an eventual civil rights icon. She spoke about her experience publicly, corresponded with friends about it privately, and recorded thoughts she kept to herself. Beyond that, she wrote movingly about a world weighted against African Americans and women. Through these cathartic writings, shown in her own hand here for the first time in print, Parks navigated, and coped with, the malignancy of oppression. As such, these manuscripts, with their "intimacies of the past life," further illuminate what was for Parks "the dark closet of my mind," a way of life that "was like walking a tightrope across a bottomless pit," and her "determination to go on with the task of becoming free—not only for ourselves, but for the nation and the world."

Is it worthwhile to reveal the intimacies of the past life? Would the people be sympathetic or disillusioned when the facts of my life are told? Would they be interested or indifferent? Would the results be harmful or good?

Rosa McCauley with a friend, ca. 1928, Pine Level, Alabama. A former classmate wrote to her in 1929: "I just bet anything the boys in your classes can't get their lessons for looking at you. I know the majority of them likes you, they can't help it. (How about it?) You say you are only in love with books, but you can't fool me."

CHAPTER 1   Early Life and Activism

Age six was a defining year in the long life of Rosa Louise McCauley. She had started first grade in a rickety one-room schoolhouse for black children, completed her first quilt, mastered basic cooking, and worked as a field hand picking cotton, planting corn, and milking cows. She also stood guard with her shotgun-wielding grandfather as the "KKK moved through the country burning negro churches, schools, flogging and killing." It was 1919, and black soldiers back from the Great War in Europe wanted their rights as citizens and respect for their service, two of many things white society had little intention of granting. Race riots broke out around the country, and a resurgent Ku Klux Klan, armed with torches and lynch ropes, terrorized the South. The lessons imparted that year remained with her, manifesting themselves in a relentless work ethic and a commitment to fighting injustice.

Given her responsibilities as a six-year-old, she "never had a whole lot of leisure time just to play." After leaving her public schoolhouse to attend a private school on scholarship, she spent her afternoons cleaning classrooms, assisting with household chores, and helping an ill aunt with her work at a Jewish country club. "There were times when we would go just walking along the roadside through the woods . . . and pick berries. And occasionally we would, if enough of us children could get together and we'd have a little time, we might play a little ball. . . . I used to go fishing with my grandmother a great deal and I rather enjoyed that . . . then we'd have some fish for supper when we got home." A good student, she left school at sixteen to care for her ailing mother and grandmother and worked for a time as a domestic as the Great Depression set in.

A life with many roles and few respites was well under way long before young Rosa McCauley, who did housework, became Rosa Parks, a household name.

I stayed awake many nights, keeping vigil with Grandpa. I wanted to see him kill a Ku Kluxer. He declared the first to invade our home would surely die.

In a few terse lines of written recollections, Rosa Parks sketched the hardships her family, like so many others she knew in rural Alabama, lived and dealt with: "Life of extreme poverty because father left mother when I was 2½ years old, and before my brother's birth. Semi invalid . . . grandparents (mother's parents) tried to care for us while mother worked as a rural school teacher as sole support of the family. The meager income supplemented by working small farm and hired for day work on other people's farms, at .50 to .75 and very rarely $1 per day. Early morning until night."

Rosa found bright spots in voracious reading, school friends, and a teenage romance, although a former classmate, Galatas, wondered in a letter from 1928: "Who do you go with now? Are you and Lee Earnest still angry with each other? I didn't think you and him would ever bust up, you all were getting along so good." She also drew strength in the African Methodist Episcopal (AME) church. Sundays and church services were "events that I could look forward to. I have always liked to attend church . . . all the people in the church would be singing and praying. I can remember enjoying hymns, singing hymns . . . it was just a part of my life."

Through a mutual friend in 1931 she met Raymond Parks, a barber, who would become her husband the following year. She was impressed with his intelligence and his polite and gentle manner; the fact that he was one of the few men she knew who drove his own car also worked in his favor. He supported her return to the classroom, and in 1933 she earned her high school diploma. And it was Raymond, ten years her senior and long active in civil rights issues, who helped her channel her anger over injustice into an organized effort to fight it.

The McCauley family home in Tuskegee, Alabama, where Rosa Louise McCauley was born, February 4, 1913.

Early Childhood
Incidents and experiences

Deserted by father at 2½ years, shortly before brother's birth. Mother was with her semi invalid parents Greatgrand father's playing with my brother and me.. He was an ex-slave of Scotch - Irish desent, African ancestry either remote or non existant It died when I was six years old. Mother Taught school in the rural community where we lived. KKK moved through the country burning Negro Churches, schools, flogging and killing. Grandfather stayed up to wait for them to come to our house. He kept his shot gun within hand reach at all times. My aunt, a widow, and her five small children came to our house at night. We could not undress and go to bed at night. The doors and windows were boarded and nailed tight from the inside. I stayed awake many

The Percivals of Pine Level, Alabama, feature prominently in this family bible. They were Rosa's maternal grandmother's family, descended from James Percival (ca. 1830–1920), a Scotch-Irish indentured servant, and his wife, Mary Jane Nobles (ca. 1843–1916), a slave of wholly African descent. The first three of their nine children were born into slavery, including Rosa's grandmother, Rosena Percival Edwards (1859–1929), for whom she was named.

FAMILY RECORD

1900
1910

Name.	Place of Birth.
C. B. Percival	Pine Level
C. Beatress Sherman	
Mabel Percival	Montgomery Ala.
Nathaniel Russville	Pine Level Ala.
Johnnie Sherman	Pine Level Ala.
Harmon Russville	Pine Level Ala.
Helen Russville	Pine Level Ala
Leona Edwards	Pine Level, Montg. Alabama.
Howard Williamson	Pine Level, Montg. Ala.
Nathaniel Percival	Pine Level, Ala.
Eugene Percival	Pine Level, Ala.
Robert Percival	Pine Level, Ala.
John Henry Sherman	Pine Level, Ala.
H. C. Sherman	Pine Level, Ala.
Leon Percival	Pine Level, Ala.
David Weatherly	Romer Ala.
Willis Freud Arbury	Romer Ala.
Minnie Lee Arbury	Romer Ala.
Willis James Arbury	Montgomery Ala.
Bessie Arbury	Pine Level, Ala.

FAMILY RECORD

Date of Birth.	Date of Marriage.	Date of Death.
		Dec-22-1939
Jan 7 1903		Pearl Albury
Nov 11 1900		
Aug 2 1904		H C Albury
April 2 1906		R C Sherman
April 26 1906		Feb-2 8-1936
Dec. 16 '88		
Aug. 10, 86		
April 2, 88. 1888	April 18, 1912	
Nov 1908		
April 2nd 1906		
January 14th 1908		
March 18th 1911		
April 26th 1906		
November 12th 1908		
October 2nd 1896		
Nov - 2 4 - 1918		
March 2 1915		
April 1918		
Jan - 16 - 1941		
Sept - 2 - 1911		

Leona Edwards McCauley (mother of Rosa), seated, and her cousin, Beatrice Brooks, 1925. Parks would later write, "My mother was a very beautiful woman and a good mother to us, also a devoted daughter of her own parents. She was attractive to men and there was one, I was so fond of that I wanted him for my father. He was a tall, handsome bachelor who was found murdered mysteriously. . . . I don't know what their relationship was or might have been; his death was a great loss to me."

Rosa's father, James McCauley, 1925. Writing from Modesto, California, in 1950, he told her: "I kept thinking of writing you, and still putting it off. It was in view of the fact that I was overshadowed with open shame that I and I alone allowed the evil spirit to lead me completely out of myself for these many years in gross desertion of a good wife and two of the sweetest children ever lived. And at a time when I was needed most. I dread to mention these unpleasant events to you but as I am now on the sunset side of life I need to unburden myself of these sins of such cruel nature. I sometimes think they are unforgiveable." He signed his letter "James."

Parks wrote on the back of this photograph, "To cousin Minnie, from Rosa L. Parks," probably about 1933. Minnie Lee Arbury was the daughter of Pearlie Percival Arbury and Henry Arbury.

Sylvester J. McCauley, Parks's brother, served in the U.S. Army in both Europe and the Pacific during World War II. She wrote of their childhood: "I adored my brother and never wanted him to get a whipping for being naughty. . . . It seemed that I received more whippings for not 'telling on him' than for doing things myself that may have provoked punishment." McCauley (known as "Brother" in the family) returned from the war expecting better treatment following his military service— just as black veterans of World War I had—but it was not forthcoming. He moved to Detroit and left the South for good.

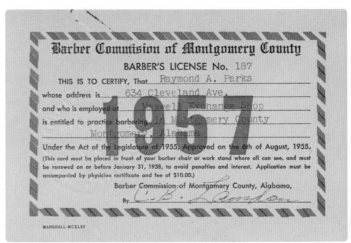

Raymond Parks's barber's license,
Montgomery County, 1957.

Raymond Parks, ca. 1947. Like his wife, Raymond was
abandoned as a young child by his father, a carpenter.
Raymond struggled as a light-skinned black boy in an
all-white neighborhood, and his mother taught him
at home since the local school would not enroll him.
Rosa found him bright and a pleasure to talk with, but
she also initially thought he was "too white" for her.

Raymond Parks, second from left, outside
Atlas Barber & Beauty, Montgomery, ca. 1947.

On the back of NAACP letterhead from 1956, Rosa Parks wrote a remarkable statement: "I would rather be lynched than live to be mistreated."

She continued:

When I was a very little girl, not more than ten years old, I angrily cried these words to my grandmother in answer to a severe scolding she gave me. I happened to quite casually mention that a white boy had met me in the road some days before and had said he would hit me. He made a threatening gesture with his fist at the same time he spoke. I picked up a small piece of brick and drew back to strike him if he should hit me. I was angry, though he seemed to be half teasing and half bullying me. He went his way without further comment.

Perhaps he never thought of it again. I don't why I remembered to mention it later to Grandma . . . as we were alone in the kitchen. To me she was the most wonderful person alive. I loved her dearly to the end of her life. I always like[d] talking things over with her and told her most everything.

I was not at all prepared for her stern reprimand of, "Gal, you had better learn that white folks is white folks and how to talk and not talk to them. You better stop being so high strung or you will be lynched before you get grown. I'm mighty scared you won't live to be grown if you don't learn not to talk biggity to white folks."

I was stunned, shocked, hurt and angered beyond anything I had ever felt. At that moment, I learned my first and hardest lesson in race relations. I felt that I was completely alone, without a friend. The one I held most dear had become an enemy, aligned with the hostile white race against me.

I cried bitterly that I would be lynched rather than be run over by them. They could get the rope ready for me any time they wanted to do their lynching.

While my neck was spared of the lynch rope and my body was never riddled by bullets or dragged by an auto, I felt that I was lynched many times in mind and spirit. I grew up in a world of white power used most cruelly and cunningly to suppress poor helpless black people.

In several of her handwritten notes and recollections, Parks likened navigating the complexities and dangers of segregation to constantly walking on a tightrope or performing acrobatics. Segregation was intended not only to keep blacks and whites separate but to keep blacks subjugated through outright violence, added hardships, and continual indignities. Parks wrote of paying one's fare at the front of a bus, then having to get off to board it again at the rear entrance, and being told at the downtown public library that the book one wanted was there but that "the requested book will be sent to the colored branch library." In her investigations for the NAACP, she described a school superintendent who opposed buses for black

OPPOSITE: In this undated manuscript, Parks gives an account of working as a teenage domestic and fending off the unwanted advances of a white man who "was fast becoming intoxicated on alcohol and lustful desire for my body." The eleven-page piece uses extensive dialogue in which Parks lays bare the contorted logic of what she called elsewhere "Daytime Segregation and Nighttime Integration." "He need not think that because he was a low-down, dirty dog of a white man and I was a poor, defenseless helpless colored girl that he could run over me," she wrote. "If he wanted to kill me and rape a dead body, he was welcome, but he would have to kill me first, and I would no longer be responsible for myself." Parks notes that the incident occurred "in the late spring of 1931, I was past my 18th birthday." Through her later work as branch secretary with the NAACP, Parks regularly investigated sexual assault cases and counseled women who had been trapped in similar situations.

one whom I trusted and thought was a friend. I felt filthy and stripped naked of every shred of decency. In a flash of a moment I was no longer a decent, self respecting teen age girl, but a flesh pot, strumpet to be bargained for and parceled as a commodity from Negro to white man.

My puny 5 foot 2", 120 lb frame could not possibly be pitted against this tall, heavy set man. He seemed at least 6" tall, weighing possibly 200 pounds. He was young, strikingly handsome, with very black hair, and dark, swarthy color of skin. He was fast becoming intoxicated on alchohol and lustful desire for my body.

So many frantic thoughts raced through my mind. His strength—my weakness physically—The white man's dominance over the Negro's submissive

Men gathered in front of a market in Montgomery, Alabama, in 1939. Signs in the window offer pig tails and chitterlings—and for fifteen cents a pound, "good steak." At the time, Parks was working with the NAACP on the "Scottsboro Boys" case.

students even though they had farther to travel to school than white children, who received public transportation. "It is not easy to remain rational and normal mentally in such a setting," she concluded.

Just as challenging as segregation's inherent inequity was its inconsistent application, which underscored how indefensible the entire system was. Parks wrote: "In our airport in Montgomery, there is a white waiting room, none for colored except an unmarked seat in the entrance. It doesn't say who should take this seat. There are restroom facilities for white ladies and colored women, white men and colored men. We stand outside after being served at the same ticket counter instead of sitting on the inside. Also there is only one drinking fountain. We board the plane and find no segregation. On arrival in [Birmingham], we note one waiting room, but white and colored drinking fountains."

In contemplating the insidious nature of racial oppression, Parks wrote: "We soothe ourselves with the salve of attempted indifference, accepting the false pattern set up by the horrible restriction of Jim Crow laws. Let us look at Jim Crow for the criminal he is and what he had done to one life multiplied millions of times over these United States and the world." She was especially bothered that in Montgomery, "where segregation was the order of the day," it was a "way of life and accepted pattern apparently taken for granted by all with the exception of few persons who were called radicals, sore heads, agitators, troublemakers, to name just a few terms given them. The masses seemed not to put forth too much effort to struggle against the status quo." For Parks herself, her position was "never to accept it, even if it must be endured." At one point, however, she believed, "There was no solution for us who could not easily conform to this oppressive way of life." Yet her whole life, it seems, would be spent fighting back, looking for that solution. Her purpose, she wrote, was to "search for a way of working for freedom and first class citizenship."

"Separate but equal" drinking fountains in the segregated South.

Students playing basketball at Prairie Farms, an all-black resettlement community for farm families established during the Great Depression, Montgomery, 1939.

Undated notebook page, ca. 1956.

Living in the deep south where Legally enforced racial segregation in all areas of life was like walking a tight rope across a bottomless pit. There was no solution for us who could not ~~could~~ easily conform, to to this oppressive way of life.

Students in school at Prairie Farms, Montgomery, 1939. "The schools in the south were the best training ground for teaching Negro inferiority and white supremacy," Parks wrote in an undated manuscript. "A young child starting to school could very soon learn that the white children went to beautiful well-appointed and equipped school buildings while Negro children went to roughly built, uncomfortable shacks, with no desks, but rough plank benches. . . . It was very rare for a young Negro to look forward to finishing his education [and] entering a well-paying profession. The teachers were poorly prepared as well as underpaid."

Not surprisingly, Rosa Parks pinpointed "early childhood" as the origin of her frustration over segregation and racism. Reading up on the NAACP and the "histories of others—Crispus Attucks, through all wars—Richard Allen, Dr. Adam Clayton Powell, women—[Phillis] Wheatley, Sojourner Truth, Harriet Tubman, Mary McLeod Bethune" was inspiring and helped focus her thoughts. Raymond introduced her to the "Scottsboro Boys" case, which he had thrown himself into shortly after nine black youth, from thirteen to twenty years old, were falsely accused of raping two white women in 1931. Organizing on their behalf, Raymond visited them in prison and was part of an underground group working to defend them. (Eight were convicted and condemned to death.) It was dangerous work, and the Parkses hosted meetings at their home that could have ended in tragedy had they been found out. She noted that "the police had killed two men who were connected" with Raymond's efforts to free the men.

In 1943 Parks joined the NAACP's Montgomery chapter and began serving as its secretary. She also advised the affiliated youth group and was regularly sent to investigate "cases of police brutality, rape, murder, countless others." In her autobiography Parks, perhaps out of modesty, greatly downplayed her role in seeking justice for victims. The running theme of racial sexual violence, by white men against black women, figured greatly in her work as she met with numerous victims and took their testimonies, though "it was terribly hard getting people to come forward with what they knew." Sexual assaults, notably two abduction and gang rape cases, brought together activists from the Scottsboro campaign, the NAACP, and other groups, who then went public, with news reports first appearing in the black press. Outraged by what she had learned from investigating a gang rape

in Abbeville in 1944, Parks cofounded the Committee for Equal Justice for Mrs. Recy Taylor and arranged for Taylor to find housing and work in Montgomery. State officials blamed the uproar over Taylor, a young mother and sharecropper, on communist agitators, and none of the perpetrators, who offered to pay off Taylor's husband, were punished.

Parks also formed the Citizens' Committee for Gertrude Perkins in 1949 in a similar case, in which the two rapists were police officers, who also were not charged. Such attacks were, as Parks and other black women knew, all too common. Although segregation, discrimination, and voter registration had received the most attention from civil rights activists, it was the concerted effort to prosecute rape cases, the thorniest of all, that laid much of the organizational groundwork for the Montgomery Bus Boycott and, by extension, the modern civil rights movement. Parks, though she would not say so herself, was among those at the center of that groundwork.

Parks's work for the NAACP nearly amounted to a full-time job, in addition to others she held as a seamstress, office clerk, and nanny. In 1941 she began work at Maxwell Field, a U.S. military base, where she marveled at being in an integrated setting. Four years later, she left Alabama for the first time in her life to attend an NAACP leadership conference in Atlanta run by Ella Baker. Her gradual friendships with white civil rights workers and allies, such as Virginia and Clifford Durr, and her attendance at the Highlander Folk School workshop on school desegregation in 1955 further encouraged in her the notion that progress toward an integrated society might be possible. "I was forty-two years old," she said of her Highlander experience, "and it was one of the few times in my life up to that point when I did not feel any hostility from white people."

Parks, right, with Septima Clark, a civil rights activist and the director of workshops at the integrated Highlander Folk School in Monteagle, Tennessee. In August 1955 Parks attended a two-week session on implementing the *Brown v. Board of Education* decision to integrate public schools, one of a number of pioneering courses Clark developed to train social justice activists. It was at Highlander that Parks learned new strategies and techniques she would employ during the Montgomery Bus Boycott.

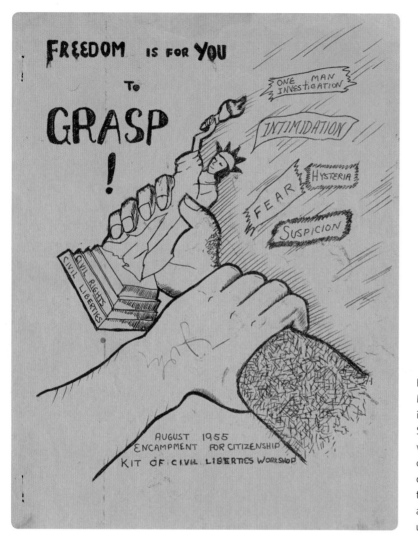

Parks attended Highlander at the height of the McCarthy era, when civil liberties were violated in an effort to identify communists in the United States. Her copy of *Freedom Is for You to Grasp!*, a workshop booklet, covered current civil liberties cases nationwide as well as programs to educate citizens about their constitutional rights, how to work with established rights organizations, and action items Highlander participants could undertake when they returned home.

OPPOSITE: Passengers standing under their respective signs begin boarding buses to destinations throughout the South.

Raymond and Rosa Parks, third and fourth from left, likely at an NAACP branch meeting, ca. 1947.

Clarence Norris, one of the nine "Scottsboro Boys" who was falsely accused and convicted of rape in 1931, leaves Montgomery's Kilby Prison after being paroled in 1946. The Parkses had worked for the defense and followed the case closely over the years. Rosa's own verdict in the matter was succinct: "The whole Scottsboro ordeal was a travesty of justice. It's a monument to America at its worst."

For Collection Period Beginning Oct. 1, 1956 and Ending on Feb. 1, 1957

POLL TAX RECEIPT

COUNTY OF MONTGOMERY, ALA., *1-21-* 1957   N°   2425

RECEIVED OF *Rosa Louise Parks*   Male ☐   Female ☒

_____ Dollars ($ *1⁵⁰*)

For Poll Taxes at $1.50 per year for the following years: 1956 (✓)   1957 ( )

District No._____ Precinct No. This Year *3N* Precinct No. Last Year_____ Color *Col*

Countersigned By

John Draues
State Comptroller.   _____ Tax Collector

Parks's poll tax receipt, January 21, 1957.
She was finally registered to vote in 1945,
at age thirty-two, on her third attempt,
but was still required to pay eleven years'
worth of poll taxes, retroactive to the
voting age of twenty-one.

Parks kept a collection of political and
labor union pins, including these in
support of workers in the aluminum,
aircraft, gas, and chemical industries.

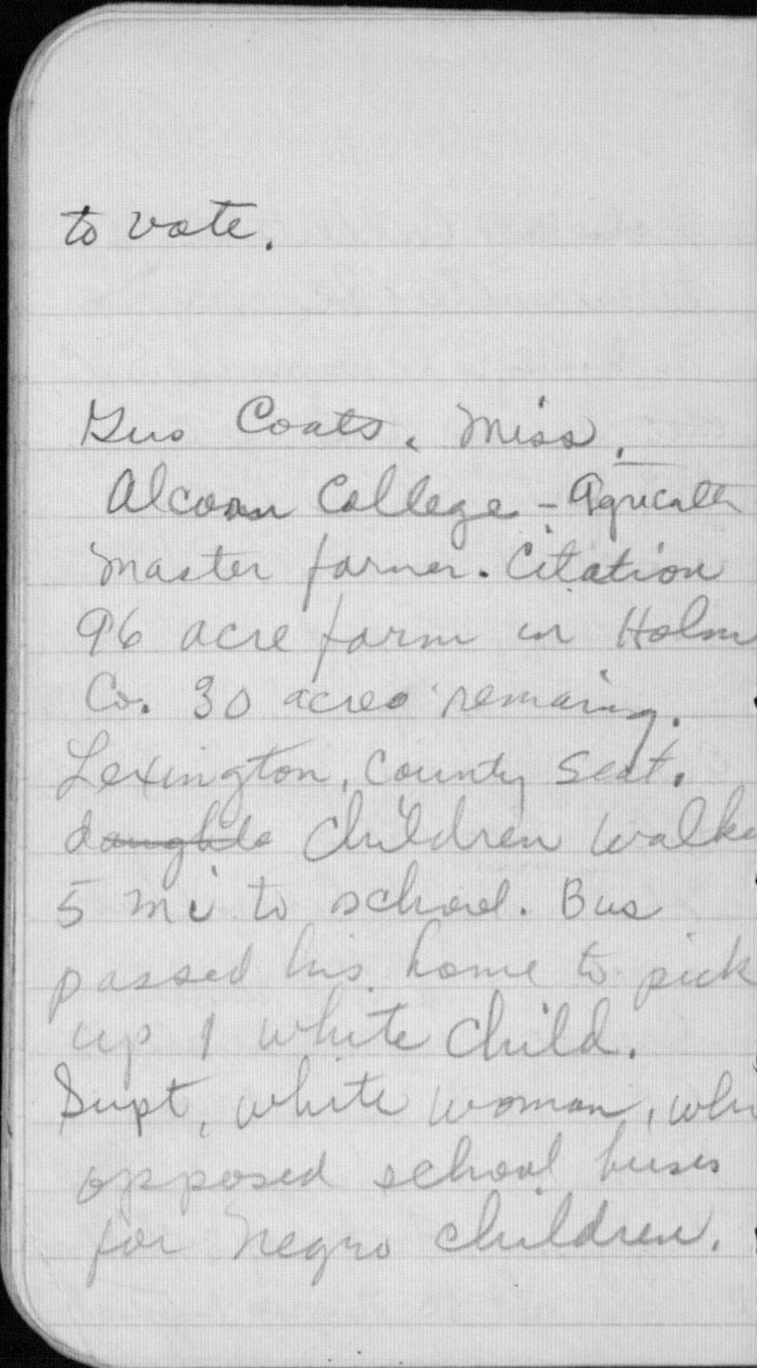

to vote.

Gus Coats, Miss,
Alcorn College - Agricult
master farmer. Citation
96 acre farm in Holm
Co. 30 acres remaining.
Lexington, county seat.
daughter children walke
5 mi to school. Bus
passed his home to pick
up 1 white child.
Supt, white woman, who
opposed school buses
for negro children.

Parks investigated civil rights cases for the NAACP on a range of issues. On the pages shown here, she took notes on a superintendent who prevented black children from riding the bus to school.

Reason white ppl may resent.
She said as long as she
was supt, no negro children
would ride school buses.

Threatened by white share cropper
for getting ppl to register.
planned to steal his cattle

Some were stolen - returned
sold land and cattle
moved to Delta.
Umpshaw Co, refused
registration there.
Brought court action.
Sheriff asked for opportunity
to open books

FIRST TIME IN BALTIMORE!

HEAR!— # MRS. ROSA PARKS

Whose arrest, because she refused to be segregated, led to the Bus Boycott in Montgomery, Alabama.

BALTIMORE BRANCH N.A.A.C.P.

KICK-OFF
MASS MEETING

SUNDAY, SEPTEMBER 23, 1956 - 3 P.M.

SHARP STREET METHODIST CHURCH

Dolphin and Etting Streets

—Music by Famous **BALTIMORE CHORALE**—

under direction of Gerald Burkes Wilson

RENEW YOUR MEMBERSHIP TODAY!
And Get One More!

Good Music   *Admission Free*

Mrs. Lillie M. Jackson, President   Dr. Charles Watts, Treasurer

A flyer advertises Parks's appearance in Baltimore to speak about the bus boycott. In raising money for the NAACP and the Montgomery Improvement Association, she accepted only expenses and donated whatever else she received. Her boycott work took a serious toll on both her physical and financial health.

CHAPTER 2   ## The Bus Boycott

Rosa Parks was certainly not the first person to defy laws that relegated black passengers to the back of city buses or required them to give up their seats to white riders. Nor was she the second or the third; she was much further down a lengthy list of resisters from Montgomery alone, not to mention the rest of the South. Her predecessors had been shouted at, beaten up, arrested, and threatened or shot at by drivers armed with nightsticks, guns, and police powers. During World War II, the U.S. Army court-martialed a young officer for causing a stir after he loudly refused to move to the rear of a bus trundling around Ft. Hood, Texas. Lieutenant Jack Robinson was acquitted, and three years later, out of khakis and in a Dodgers jersey, he would break Major League Baseball's color barrier.

In Montgomery in 1949, Professor Jo Ann Robinson, president of the Women's Political Council (WPC) and an instructor at Alabama State College, first studied and discussed the feasibility of staging a bus boycott, having also suffered the indignities that came with her bus fare. The WPC, other women's clubs, and the NAACP petitioned and complained to the city about abusive drivers to no effect. Finding the will to support a bus boycott was difficult, however, since blacks who fought back faced a catalog of consequences, from immediate violence to a subsequent loss of employment and the hardship that would follow. As Parks noted, both blacks and whites were "conditioned" to segregation, making progress that much harder to achieve. Black women—the largest percentage of bus riders—received the brunt of mistreatment from profanity-spewing white drivers, who occasionally passed them by at bus stops or drove off before they could board.

The tipping point came in the mid-1950s, after generations of activism, court cases, and negotiations. It was fueled by a quick series

I felt if I did not resist being mistreated that I would spend the rest of my life being mistreated.

of high-profile events, beginning with the landmark U.S. Supreme Court ruling in *Brown v. Board of Education* in May 1954 that declared racially segregated public schools unconstitutional. Then, in March 1955, fifteen-year-old Claudette Colvin was roughed up, dragged off a Montgomery bus, and arrested for refusing to give up her seat. Colvin's conviction on assault and battery charges infuriated the black community. Grief and rage nationwide followed the brutal torture-murder in August of fourteen-year-old Emmett Till in Mississippi, whose lynching brought home, perhaps as never before to those outside the Bible Belt, the true nature of Jim Crow.

In the midst of these events, in Montgomery, the original capital of the Confederacy, Jo Ann Robinson and the WPC drew up ready-to-implement bus boycott plans should the opportunity arise, and she warned Mayor William Gayle that they would act if conditions did not improve. Churchgoers rallied behind their pastors, including two young action-minded Baptist ministers, Ralph Abernathy, age twenty-nine, and Martin Luther King Jr., age twenty-six, who were calling for racial justice. The well-connected, indefatigable E. D. Nixon, president of the local NAACP chapter and a veteran union organizer, was aching to act in the glare of a national spotlight. And newly minted attorney Fred Gray, barred from law school in his home state, had recently returned from Ohio, pausing only to hang out his shingle before plunging into a stack of civil rights cases. So in December, when "gentle," "respectable" Parks was arrested, jailed, convicted, and fined for remaining in her window seat on a municipal bus, organizers immediately responded, and Montgomery's black citizens rose up.

Ku Klux Klan members abducted, tortured, and murdered Emmett Till, age fourteen (seen here with his mother, Mamie Bradley), in Money, Mississippi, in August 1955, after a white woman falsely claimed he had grabbed at her. The gruesome killing directed national attention to the South's brutal system of Jim Crow. Parks said that Till was on her mind when, several months later, she refused to give up her bus seat in Montgomery.

On Thursday evening, December 1, Rosa Parks walked from the downtown Montgomery Fair department store, where she worked as a seamstress, to Court Square to catch the Cleveland Avenue bus. When it arrived, she took a seat behind the front section reserved for whites. At the next stop, outside the Empire Theater, white riders got on, and since the front rows had filled, one man was left standing. Driver James Blake ordered Parks and three others in the same row to give up their seats and make way for the new white passenger. Three of them reluctantly obeyed Blake. Parks did not. She had not boarded that bus looking for a fight; instead, she later wrote, "If I had been paying attention, I wouldn't even have gotten on that bus." Ever since she'd had a run-in with Blake a dozen years before, she had avoided his buses. But she, too, had reached her tipping point.

The resulting conversation lasted only a few seconds:

Blake: "Are you going to stand up?"
Parks: "No."
Blake: "Well, I'm going to have you arrested."
Parks: "You may do that."

Jane Gunter, a young, pregnant, white military wife new to Montgomery, unfamiliar with local bus practice and seated directly behind the driver, began to stand and said, "She can take my seat." Instantly, a tall, thin white man approached her, pushed against her with his knees, and whispered, "Don't you make a move!" She sat down, stunned. Blake ordered everyone off the bus and went to a payphone to summon the police. As the off-loaded passengers gathered on the sidewalk, Gunter fled on foot,

but Parks remained in her seat until two officers arrived and took her into custody without incident. "I felt just resigned to give what I could to protest against the way I was being treated," she said later. "And I felt that all of our meetings, trying to negotiate, bring about petitions before the authorities, that is the city officials, really hadn't done any good at all."

Word of Parks's arrest ricocheted all over town. The next day, she took a cab to work. Her unblemished reputation and her calm demeanor prompted Nixon to instantly choose her as the face of resistance and the plaintiff in a test case on the legality of bus segregation. Over the weekend, it was agreed that a one-day bus boycott would be held on Monday, and ministers spread the word during Sunday church services. Thousands of handbills about the boycott were mimeographed and distributed. The one-day rider strike was so successful that at a standing-room-only meeting that evening at Holt Street Baptist Church, black leaders asked if the boycott should continue. "The atmosphere was very, I would say practically jubilant," Parks recalled, "because people were singing, clapping their hands and shouting, and doing all that kind of thing. . . . People were just yelling out that they would remain off the buses until changes were made for the better." With that, the Montgomery Improvement Association (MIA) was established to manage a continued boycott, King was named its president, and Parks agreed to serve on the board. She accepted the risks that would come with being such a visible figure in the boycott, and her case quickly escalated from a local incident to national news and from a momentary act to an actual movement.

No. *41464*   The City of Montgomery   Recorder's Court

Rosa Parks   vs.   *Dec 5*   19*55*

The defendant   appeared in open court, in *own*
proper person   ; the case was heard, and the defendant   *was* found   guilty and
fined   *10.00* dollars and cost, and in default of
payment of the fine and costs *was* sentenced to
hard labor for the City   *14*
days

Jno B. Scal Recorder

appealed

I CERTIFY. That the foregoing is a correct transcript from the docket of the cause in the **RECORDER'S COURT**, which with the original papers in cause, I herewith transmit to your Honorable Court.

Judge Frank M. Johnson
To the Clerk of the Circuit Court M. C.

Clerk of Recorder's Court.

Parks's court record shows that four days after her arrest, she appeared before a judge who found her guilty of violating city law and fined her ten dollars. That morning, the boycott had begun, and Parks was gratified and thrilled to see the buses passing by with virtually no passengers.

I had been pushed around ~~for~~ all my life ~~here~~ and felt at this moment that I could'nt take it anymore. When I asked the policeman why we ~~were~~ had to be pushed around? He said he did'nt know. "The law is the law. You are under arrest." ~~A acta I went with~~ I did'nt resist.

He was a mad man. Furious.
His fury was directed at himself
for being a financial failure.
Not having provided the material
comforts necessary for a well —
appointed home.

He was angry with the driver for
causing my arrest. He mentioned so
often the fact that col people were
sitting on this same seat, the
next day and all the other days,
where I was arrested for not
getting up. He was also very angry
with me for refusing to give up
the seat and at least getting off
the bus. So many times he said he
would have gotten off the bus. He
said I had a "goat head."

Finally he was angry with the
Negroes of the community for not taking
mass action earlier in the Claudette
Colvin case in particular. There were
many good opportunities for mass action
long before Dec 1, 1955.

Shortly after her act of
defiance, Parks described
and speculated on the
explosive reaction of her
husband, Raymond,
to her arrest.

The Montgomery Bus Boycott demands were few and simple but proved impossible for the city's white commissioners to grant:

1. Bus drivers behave in a civil manner.
2. Change to a first-come, first-served seating policy that still placed white riders in the front and blacks in the back.
3. Hire African American drivers.

Asked by a television reporter what the protesters hoped to gain, Parks summed up their goal concisely: "Well, we hope to achieve equal rights as any human being deserves. That's what we're working for." So the boycott continued. Nightclub manager Rufus Lewis managed the motor pool as an army of volunteer drivers picked up and dropped off tens of thousands of passengers daily at designated points around the city. Parks worked for a time as a dispatcher, scheduling drivers and arranging rides. Black churches, business associations, and women's clubs contributed to the effort, resulting in a fleet of more than twenty newly purchased and donated station wagons. The carpool system became so reliable that Nixon declared, "It works better than the Montgomery City Lines." Although it cost more than $300 each day in gas and oil to keep the boycott running, it cost the bus company $3,000 each day in lost ridership.

White Montgomery was not willing to give up its privileges, but black Montgomery willingly gave up a great deal to maintain its protest. "Beginning at 5 am, one can see people trudging in from the country from as far as seven miles away, walking to work," reported the *Chicago Defender*, the most prominent black newspaper in the country. As part of Mayor Gayle's "get tough" stance, black cab drivers were prohibited from charging lower rates to protesters; volunteer drivers lost their car insurance; and Parks, King, and nearly ninety others were arrested in February for violating a law against boycotts. In her notes on the crackdown, Parks wrote that "policemen began arresting drivers—forbidding white employers [from] transporting help. Several persons have been fired from [their] jobs for not riding the buses. Some for driving in the pool." She also made note that drivers sometimes missed meals and were "wearing out their cars, bought at great sacrifice." In January, King's house was bombed and other leaders' homes were also dynamited. Both Parks and her husband lost their jobs. She was discharged from hers, and he resigned from his when his boss banned any mention of his wife or the boycott in the barbershop. ("I worked five long, tense weeks with people who never spoke to me even once after the bus incident," she wrote shortly afterward.) Along with other notable figures in the protest, Parks was on the receiving end of continual death threats on the phone and hate letters in her mailbox. As her grandfather had done before when threatened, her husband took to keeping a gun on hand at night.

Among the white population, well-to-do women also had to make adjustments if they wanted their household employees on the job first thing in the morning. City officials, the White Citizens' Council, and angry neighbors were unable to stop many of them from being what amounted to inadvertent volunteers in an auxiliary corps of the motor pool. "Even more astonishing is the sight of sleepy-eyed white women, some with their hair still rolled up in pin curls, chauffeuring their nursemaids and cooks," wrote Ethel Payne of the *Chicago Defender*. "Since a large proportion of Montgomery's Negro population is domestically employed, the reaction of the white women is very significant. This is a reflection of the Southern way of life where the sheltered white woman is as much dependent upon Negro help for her leisurely living as they are dependent upon her for a living. . . . The backbone of the movement are the domestics." As a former domestic herself, Parks knew this as well as anyone.

The movement in Montgomery was soon traveling on two different routes to a common destination. On city streets, the boycott plowed on, having drawn worldwide news coverage and its participants determined to see it through. In the courts, Parks's appeal failed and her conviction stood, but attorney Fred Gray seamlessly moved to Plan B. Four other women—Aurelia Browder, Claudette Colvin, Susie McDonald, and Mary Louise Smith—all mistreated bus passengers (like Colvin, Smith also had been arrested), signed on to participate in what became a pivotal lawsuit, *Browder v. Gayle*. They sued the city, with Gray arguing that bus segregation violated their Fourteenth Amendment rights. In its defense, the city claimed it was merely upholding state law. At the intersection of the bus boycott and the women's lawsuit, the crusade that dared to reckon with Jim Crow was well under way.

Parks's notes and draft instructions for riders during the boycott. She urged carpool passengers to have patience, asking that they "remember how long some of us had to wait when the buses passed us without stopping."

OPPOSITE: Parks packed a lot of detail into a brief letter on January 31, 1956, to her brother as the bus boycott neared the end of its second month. As this short missive indicates, Parks, who had just lost her job, spent nearly all her time dealing with the protest.

6

Dear Brother:

How are you and the family? I hope you are all doing fine.

We are doing quite well. I am sorry not to written you about what is going on here with our bus protest. It is just so hard for me to concentrate on writing letters.

We are really in the thick of it now. Rev. King's home was bombed last night while we were at the First Baptist Church mass meeting. His wife and baby were in the house, but not hurt.

We were interviewed and photographed by Life Magazine last Thursday. I hope you get a copy. I bought an extra copy of Jet to send you but never did get it in the mail. We were also on the Dave Garroway TV program "Today" sometime ago.

I must close for now. Write soon. Best regards to Daisy and the children.

Lovingly your sister
Rose

At Montgomery's First Baptist Church, the crowd gives a standing ovation to leaders of the bus protest following their indictment for violating a law prohibiting participation in boycotts, February 23, 1956.

E. D. Nixon, president of the local NAACP chapter, escorts Parks into the courthouse in Montgomery on March 19, 1956, for Martin Luther King Jr.'s trial after a grand jury indicted her, King, and many others for interfering with business or, as Parks described it, for having "put the bus company out of business for quite a while." Of those charged, only King was actually tried. He was found guilty but successfully appealed the verdict.

"Tote dat barge! Lift dat boycott! Ride dat bus!" On March 25, 1956, a week after Martin Luther King Jr. was tried in Montgomery, the *Washington Post* ran this Herblock cartoon of an angry white man demanding that a black man take the bus. By then, the city bus line had suffered severe financial losses.

King, Bennett, French, 1st. Nixon

Tell your friends about the Hallmark Date Book.

3rd .We'll be glad for them to have one, too!

Drivers

M. Kennedy

Name	Address	Phone No.	Birth-days	Anniver-saries	Christmas	Valentine's Day	Easter	
T. Gray	Tom Parks	Q. Murphy		L. D.	Bonner			
J. Gibson	Carlito	J. Danlile		S. P.	McBride			
W. J. Powell	W. H. John	M. Bishop		B. M.	Querhart			
A. W. Wilson diamond	J. L. Smith	C. McHone						
J. W. Hayes	E. H. Ligon	W. S. Smith						
J. H. Cherry	A. J. Hamilton	E. Posey						
	S. S. Seay		4th.					
L. C. Walker	W. Moss		J. Marrs					
M. W. Richelson	H. J. Palmer	J. H. Davis						
C. Wms.	A. Jones	H. Wms.						

While working briefly as a dispatcher during the bus boycott, Parks used this 1955 Hallmark date book to keep track of the volunteer carpool drivers who ferried former bus passengers to and from work. She also used the booklet for taking notes at various talks given by ministers and civil rights activists.

Pleading filed arrangement. Week for written

INTRODUCING

Hallmark
May Baskets

 A delightful way for children to observe the age-old tradition of delivering May Baskets to friends and loved ones.

 They will add a gay touch to Maytime parties and bring Maytime cheer to shut-ins.

 And youngsters will have lots of fun assembling and delivering Hallmark May Baskets.

Ford Local No 600 UAW-CIO.
10550 Dix ave. Dearborn, Mich

At an NAACP rally at the Second Baptist Church in Los Angeles, California, April 1956. Parks sits behind the lectern in the front row on stage. She made her first trip to the West Coast in March 1956 to speak about the ongoing Montgomery Bus Boycott and to encourage support for the growing civil rights movement.

In dashing off a quick note to her mother from New York, Rosa Parks mentioned, "I am rushing now to go to the studio to be on a radio program this morning. I have been invited to be on the Tex and Jinx show on Mutual next Friday 11:00 pm. You may hear it on WAPX or NBC or CBS 9 pm our time." Her appearance on the popular program and NBC's televised *Today Show* were part of a sustained campaign to publicize the bus boycott. The media found her compelling story and gentle comportment an intriguing combination, making her all the more in demand as a speaker and invited guest. She addressed NAACP chapters and churches from Boston to Seattle, from Los Angeles to Washington, D.C., and throughout the Midwest. Her interviews and public appearances helped keep the boycott in the news and further enhanced her effectiveness as a fund-raiser.

In her talks, Parks assured audiences that boycotters would continue to walk until they could board the buses and "ride as free men." In response, donated shoes arrived at the Montgomery NAACP office and even her own home. At one point her mother wrote to her, "Another shipment of shoes came Wednesday. . . . I have given out about eight pairs. The folks are coming in and out like bees." For a soft-spoken woman who checked out a library book to read up on public speaking, being thrust into a whirl of public engagements was a change in lifestyle, but it did not alter her measured, reserved manner. Her days and nights were filled with NAACP membership drives and meetings, rallies, luncheons and dinners, church services, and gatherings that included Thurgood Marshall, Eleanor Roosevelt, show business celebrities, and leaders she had long admired. "I suppose the people there think I will never get back to Montgomery," she wrote her mother. "Remember me to all the friends and neighbors. I have not called the numbers you sent. There just isn't time at the present." The experience was both thrilling and grueling.

Letters to her mother in this period were written on the fly or just before collapsing into bed. At many of her stops, Parks was also checking in on relatives, relaying family news back to Montgomery, and attempting to partially manage her household long distance. Raymond, wracked with worry about his wife's safety, was suffering from ulcers, and her mother became seriously ill during her absence. Mrs. McCauley sought to reassure her daughter, writing, "Do your best and I shall keep praying for you. Write when you can. . . . P.S. I have not found the tele-bill yet. The rent has been paid." In her last letter from New York, Parks told her mother, "I am leaving N.Y. now for Washington, D.C. From there I will come home. I am mailing most of my clothes by Parcel Post. They may be there by the time I get there." The next month, on June 6, 1956, the U.S. District Court for Middle Alabama ruled in *Browder v. Gayle* that bus segregation was unconstitutional. The state appealed, the boycott continued, and Parks went back on the road.

When the U.S. Supreme Court affirmed the lower court's ruling in *Browder v. Gayle* on November 13, 1956, Parks's reaction was restrained and pragmatic. She wrote on the back of a printed NAACP meeting agenda: "Today's Supreme Court decision. Happy to hear of it. We still face the local problems of implementing court decision. We are more hopeful of the future." Alabama was not done yet and asked for another hearing. So the boycott continued. "We didn't sag at all. We just kept moving on," Parks would say later. What kept her going was the mission's purpose and the fact that, as she noted, "because there were so many other people involved, I did not feel any discouragement."

More than a year after the protest began, the boycott ended in victory. The Supreme Court denied Alabama's petition, and federal marshals handed Mayor Gayle official notice of the ruling on December 20, 1956. The following day, people riding the buses in Montgomery sat anywhere they found a seat.

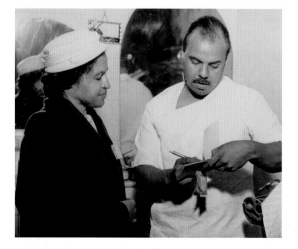

During her speaking tour out west, Parks promoted membership in the NAACP. Here she collects two-dollar membership dues.

Parks waves from a United Airlines jetway in Seattle on her cross-country travels during the boycott. The NAACP quickly recognized her value in drawing crowds and recruiting members. Her attendance at an NAACP meeting in Seattle helped bring in more than $1,400.

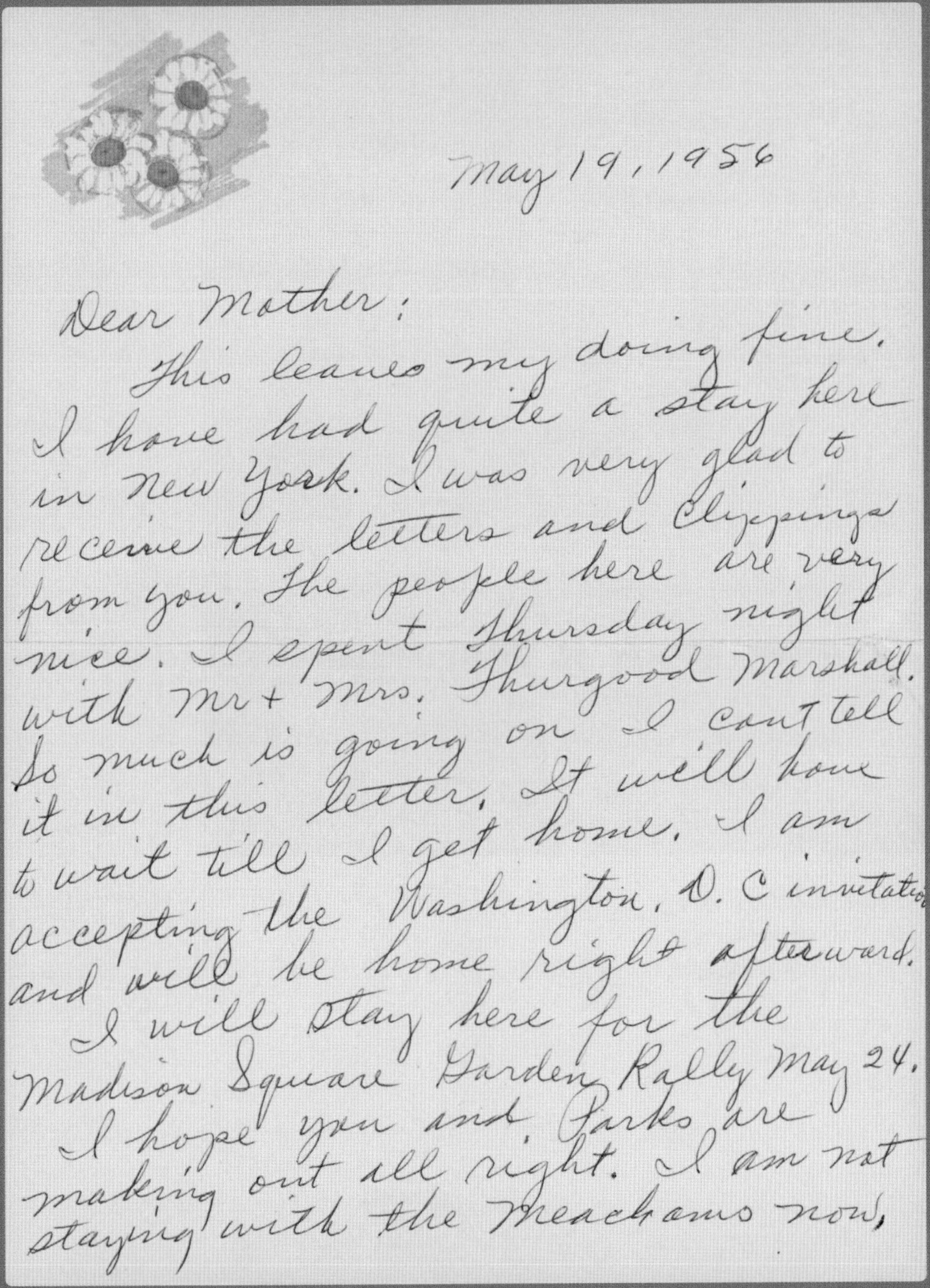

May 19, 1956

Dear Mother;

This leaves my doing fine.
I have had quite a stay here
in New York. I was very glad to
receive the letters and clippings
from you. The people here are very
nice. I spent Thursday night
with Mr + Mrs. Thurgood Marshall.
So much is going on I can't tell
it in this letter. It will have
to wait till I get home. I am
accepting the Washington, D.C invitation
and will be home right afterward.
        I will stay here for the
Madison Square Garden Rally May 24.
        I hope you and Parks are
making out all right. I am not
staying with the Meachams now.

In a letter to her mother from New York, where she maintained a hectic schedule, Parks mentions her stay with attorney (and later, the first black Supreme Court justice) Thurgood Marshall and his wife, Cecilia Suyat, a civil rights activist and secretary at NAACP headquarters.

Martin Luther King Jr., president of the Montgomery
Improvement Association, and Ralph Abernathy ride the first
desegregated bus in Montgomery on December 21, 1956, after
the 381-day boycott. Parks was taking care of her ill mother
that morning and missed the inaugural ride of a new era.

OPPOSITE: Rosa Parks, at the front of the bus.

I want to feel the nearness of something secure. It is such a lonely, lost feeling that I am cut off from life. I am nothing, I belong nowhere and to no one.

There is just so much hurt, disappointment and oppression one can take. The bubble of life grows larger. The line between reason and madness grows thinner. The re-opening of old wounds are unbearably painful.

Parks wrote of the tumult and disconnectedness she felt brought on by the boycott, her rise to prominence, and the abrupt changes in her life.

CHAPTER 3   Detroit and Beyond

Every black passenger aboard a Montgomery bus in 1957 had paid far more than bus fare to be there. For Rosa and Raymond Parks, the fight had been worth it, but staying in Montgomery was not. During the boycott, Raymond—tagged with having a "troublemaker" wife—was unable to find work. He struggled with his wife's frequent absences, the hateful calls and letters, and drinking. Rosa, in turn, under the strain of her new life, was in constant worry over his well-being, triggering a vicious circle of worsening physical health and distress for both of them. In the meantime, her brother, Sylvester McCauley, and cousin Thomas Williamson urged them to leave the South. The breaking point came that summer.

Receiving plenty of death threats but no job offers, the Parkses left their home of twenty-five years and moved to Detroit, taking Rosa's mother with them. Sylvester McCauley, who worked at the Chrysler factory, found them housing, and Williamson, who owned a cement business, financed the move. Their departure surprised and saddened many, but jealous resentment among some Montgomery civil rights activists toward Parks as an NAACP drawing card and popular figure in the black press made their decision to go less difficult. In August, after a thoughtful but somewhat awkward send-off from friends and associates, the Parkses arrived in the Motor City, ready for a new start.

Like her brother, Rosa Parks never again lived in the Deep South, but unlike him, she occasionally returned. Over the next fifty years, she would remain active in the movement, retreat from public life and reappear, and fight for new cases in the same causes she had long supported.

The only thing we can do now is not worry and have faith that the future will be better for us.

Parks had hardly settled into her new surroundings when she accepted the only paying job to come her way, as a hostess at the Holly Tree Inn, a guesthouse for the Hampton Institute, a historically black college founded after the Civil War to educate freedmen. The tremendous drawback, however, was Hampton's location at the tip of the Virginia Peninsula, nearly seven hundred miles away from Detroit by bus. The pay was decent and the work tolerable but demanding. Parks oversaw the dining room and the housekeeping staff and assisted residents and guests, often working late at night. She loved interacting with the students, faculty, and visitors but occasionally found the work dull. At one point she wrote her mother, "My social life is practically non-existent." Parks was unable to find a position there for Raymond and thus began the two years of correspondence between Detroit and Hampton that forms a large portion of her surviving handwritten letters.

A month into the job, she wrote to him:

My darling husband,
Hearing your voice this morning was such a wonderful surprise. It has made the day so pleasant for me. Of course it makes me want to see you more than ever. . . . I think of you so much and wonder how you are getting along. It is not easy for me to live alone and get along without you being near me. Also try to keep Mother cheered up and help her keep from worrying. . . . I wish you could see this place. It is beautiful and we are almost completely surrounded by water. The campus is right on the bay. There should be plenty fishing from the bank and on boats. . . . Your devoted wife, Rosa.

The burden of the past two years caught up with Parks, and on November 21, 1957, she told Raymond, "I wrote the doctor [in Detroit] for an appointment in Dec. I felt a bit painful today and I thought it best to make plans for a physical checkup. There are no decent medical facilities here. Only the Institute infirmary for students and a Jim Crow hospital called 'Dixie' which I want no part of." She was also keeping up with the happenings in Montgomery, where a newsman for the *Pittsburgh Courier* was filing a series of articles headlined, "How Has Bus Boycott Affected Montgomery Negroes?"

In assessing the events of the past year, reporter Trezzvant W. Anderson asked, "Was the Montgomery bus boycott a success? Did it do good? Or, did it hurt those who did the most to make it effective?" He observed that for Parks, such questions bring out "the bitter frustration in the heart of this noble woman who made the great sacrifice. . . . But, after her role in igniting the bus boycott, it was she who paid the price!" Anderson charged that the Montgomery Improvement Association "failed to sustain and nourish the woman who caused it all! But not once did Rosa Parks grumble or complain, and this reporter was in her house while she was packing and adjusting her things to go to Detroit to live—disillusioned and sick at heart." Parks was upset all right: "I read the two articles in [the] *Pittsburgh Courier* and felt sick over it," she wrote Raymond. "I was called by the *Chicago Defender* to make a statement. Of course, I would not say anything against the MIA."

After spending the holidays in Detroit, she returned to Hampton in January 1958, writing home, "The exray of my stomach showed an ulcer. I am on a strict milk diet (2 quarts and 1 pint of cream) with cream of wheat or oatmeal cereal for breakfast and dinner—two pieces of toast for lunch. This is taken 8 times a day along with medicine. I feel very well and am able to work. I have to buy the cream which is very expensive." Her next letter reported an improvement in health, but finances weighed on her mind, as they always had and always would: "I have to stay on the medicine for two months. It is very expensive ($5.50 for a week's supply). I am resting and sleeping much better now. . . . I want to call, but after thinking of our heavy bills and expense[s], I resist doing so." In addition to her job and tending to her health, Parks maintained her role as the family seamstress, writing, "P.S. I forgot to mention that I have put the new zipper in your jacket and will try to get it to you this week if possible. I still have to finish Brother's pants."

In a birthday card to Raymond in February, Parks noted, "My birthday was quite well remembered by those who knew of it. . . . I was not feeling too well. I must stay on the milk and soup diet one extra week longer. I am taking so much medicine. I can realize now how you must have felt in Montgomery. The same reaction you had seems to have taken a hold on me. I am keeping on the job. It is so much responsibility. This will be a month of many meetings and conferences with visitors to be looked after. I hope you are doing well in school and will continue." Later in the month, she wrote her mother: "I will go to the doctor again today. He is looking after me without charging any fee, because I am the Rosa Parks of the Montgomery bus protest. This is a great help, for the medicine is expensive." Ulcers would trouble her the rest of her life.

Back in Detroit, Raymond took classes, taught barbering, and worked as a school janitor. In March, after receiving a letter from Raymond, who preferred phone calls, Parks responded: "I was so glad to receive your letter today. I kept reading it over and over. It seems that we should not have to spend our lives so far from each other. Dearest, I wish that I did not have to be away from you a minute. I can't write just what I feel that I could say

to you. . . . I am trying hard to stay here and make good on the job. I am lonely for you even with so many other people around me. . . . I hope you are not working too hard. I am sorry you have to be away from home at night, but I hope you can get along all right, and making enough money to keep out of debt and maybe save a little."

After two years at Hampton and of separation from loved ones, Parks resigned and returned to Detroit. She would continue working as a seamstress but would not find a salary comparable to Hampton for another six years. To her, Detroit was "the promised land that wasn't." While the overt "whites only / colored only" signage was missing and segregation was not legally mandated as in Montgomery, the longtime practice of redlining—the systematic denial of financial and commercial services to those living in certain sections of the city—resulted in similarly all-black and all-white neighborhoods, churches, schools, and businesses.

In 1960, the year *Jet* magazine referred to Parks as the "bus boycott's forgotten woman," Parks, with little income and in poor health, tumbled to one of the lowest points of her life. Friends and admirers rallied to her side, but having lived a responsible, debt-free life, she found it excruciating to have her situation become public knowledge. Her interests soon turned to local issues, and as an active member of St. Matthew's, a small AME church, she visited prisoners and shut-ins and served meals; in 1965 she would become a deaconess. She also spent time with her nieces and nephews—her brother and his wife, Daisy, had thirteen children, which made for lively family gatherings. Parks continued to monitor the civil rights movement closely, and she campaigned for attorney John Conyers, an African American, during his successful run for Congress in 1964. The following spring, she began working in his Detroit office, where she would remain for more than two decades.

Jan. 9, 1958

My dear husband:

How are you? I do hope you are fine and keeping in good spirits. I am all right except for being a little tired and it is taking a little time for me to get back in the full swing of working. Everyone who knows I was under the weather is very kind and considerate. Mrs. Hamlin came back last night and kept the office open for me after dinner.

I was so happy to be home with you again. It is not easy to live alone, that is not for me. We should always be together. The only thing we can do now is not worry and have faith that the future will be better for us. I hope Mother, Brother and family are well. Please take care of yourself.

Always your loving wife,
Rosa

Gainfully employed at the Hampton Institute's Holly Tree Inn, Parks regularly sent home money to her husband and mother and managed various household affairs long distance.

OPPOSITE: Parks took a job as hostess at the Hampton Institute's guesthouse in Hampton, Virginia, shortly after the move to Detroit. She wrote of her loneliness in this note to her husband on January 9, 1958. In a letter four months later she wrote, "I would never leave you again for a job or anything else."

COMBINED UNIFORM HOUSEHOLD GOODS BILL OF LADING AND FREIGHT BILL

COAST TO COAST AUTHORITY
I.C.C. NO. MC-41098

HOWARD VAN LINES, INC.
General Office - P. O. Box 1019 - Dallas, Texas

REGIONAL OFFICES OR RESPONSIBLE AGENTS
IN ALL PRINCIPAL CITIES

Received, pursuant to Order for Services (if any) and subject to the classifications and tariffs, rules, and regulations in effect on the date of the issue of this Bill of Lading.
(Agent or Office)   (By)

Issued at (Show actual point of origin) Montgomery, Alabama   Date 8/5/57   Extended by HVL, Montgomery, Ala.   F. E. Smith

Shipper Mr. R. A. Parks   Consignee R. A. Parks

Address 634 Cleveland Court   Address 449 East Euclid Street

City & State Montgomery, Alabama   City & State Detroit, Michigan

Contact R. A. Parks   Contact R. A. Parks

ARTICLES OF EXCESS VALUATION

Description of Property—One Load Used Household Goods

TARIFF NO. 14   SEC. III   TABLE A   FOR 845 MILES ON RELEASED VALUE OF 30¢ — PER POUND PER ARTICLE.

Gross Weight 10764 lbs.   Weighed By   Location Montgomery, Alabama

Tare Weight 8850 lbs.   Weighed By   Location Montgomery, Alabama

CONSTRUCTIVE WEIGHT CERTIFICATE

	Rate	Line Haul	Ex. Pu.	Ex. Del.	Use Only	Wardrobes	Hoisting or Piano Carry	Waiting Time	Total Items At Left
Net Weight 1914 Lbs.	10.10	$212.64							212 64

SHOW AGENT OR OFFICE DUE REVENUE UNDER EACH ITEM

STORAGE IN TRANSIT   (Name of Warehouse)   (City and State)   Lbs. @   Cwt. per Mo. for   Mos. Total

DELIVERY TO OR FROM WAREHOUSE   (Name of Warehouse)   (City and State)   Lbs. @   or   Miles at   Per Cwt. Total

PLEASE NOTICE — The Regulations of the Interstate Commerce Commission require that the carrier shall not deliver or relinquish possession of any property transported by it until all tariff rates and charges have been paid in cash, money order, or cashier's check, except as rules and regulations of the Interstate Commerce Commission may otherwise prescribe.

SUB-TOTAL TAXABLE ITEMS

CONSIGNOR'S STATEMENT

Subject to Section 7 of conditions, if this shipment is to be delivered to the consignee without recourse on the consignor, the consignor shall sign the following statement:

The carrier shall not make delivery of this shipment without payment of freight and all other lawful charges, in cash or cashier's check.

Shipper or Shipper's Agent X

Shipper hereby agrees to all the terms on the face and back of this sheet, and especially agrees to accept for himself and assigns the released valuation of 30¢ per lb. per article. If more than 30¢ per lb. per article, strike out 30¢ and insert figure.

Shipper or Shipper's Agent X

Packing and Unpacking Rates Include (1) packing, unpacking, and the use of packing containers and materials, or; (2) packing and the packing containers and materials in the event that such packing containers and materials are retained by the shipper or consignee.

3% Federal Tax   6 38

DESCRIPTION		QUAN.	RATE	CHARGE
Barrels		4	6.00	24.00
Boxes, Wooden	Not Over 5 Cu. Ft.			
	Over 5 Cu. Ft., Not Over 10 Cu. Ft.			
	Over 10 Cu. Ft., Not Over 15 Cu. Ft.			

HOWARD VAN LINES, INC.

AGENT OR DRIVER

Booked by HVL, Montgomery, Alabama

Date Picked Up Aug. 19, 1957   At Res.   Whse. X

Picked Up by Owl Moving & Storage

HAULING INFORMATION

1. Lessor Owl Moving & Stg.   Pld. Eqpt. Yes / No

Driver Wm. Patterson   Orig. to dest

2. Lessor   Pld. Eqpt. Yes / No

Driver   From   To

I.C.C. AUTHORITY

1. Carrier HVL   I.C.C. NO. MC 41098

2. Carrier   I.C.C. NO. MC

	DESCRIPTION	QUAN.	RATE	CHARGE
Crates, Wooden $	Min. Minimum — Show Minimum			Ea.
Crate, No.	Over Minimum	Cu. Ft. $		Cu. Ft.
Cartons, Mirror $	Min. Minimum — Show Minimum			Ea.
Cartons, No.	Over Minimum	Cu. Ft. $		Cu. Ft.
Cartons				
	Not Over 3 Cu. Ft.	2	1.25	2.50
	Over 3 Cu. Ft., Not Over 5 Cu. Ft.	7	2.50	17.50
	Over 5 Cu. Ft., Not Over 10 Cu. Ft.			
Mattress Cartons or Bags		2	2.50	5.00
Extra Labor — Total Man Hours		Hrs. @	Hr.	
Packed by			Enter Total Packing Charges →	49 00
Transit Ins. $	@	Per M Ctf. No.	Issued By	
Advances, Other Charges (Attach Bills)				
Other Miscellaneous				

Manifest Number 21-425

2nd Manifest Number   Received Balance Payable — Carrier

X C.O.D.   Chg.   Gov't   Date Paid in full 8/23 1957   Per Driver Wm Patterson

CHARGE TO R. A. Parks   449 East Euclid St. Detroit, Michigan
(Address)   (City and State)

Services shown herein were rendered and shipment was received in good condition except as noted on Delivery Inventory.

Date of Delivery 8/23 1957   CONSIGNEE X Mrs. Rosa Parks

TOTAL		267 92
Prepayment Received		
By		
Balance		
Payable Mr. R. A. Parks		267 92

(Address)   (City and State)

BVL SD-1 10M—10-55

No. 4056

ORIGINAL — NOT NEGOTIABLE — GIVE SHIPPER WHEN LOADING — EXCEPT GOVERNMENT SHIPMENTS.

In August 1957, less than a year after the bus boycott ended, the Parkses and Leona McCauley left Alabama, relocating to Detroit, where Sylvester McCauley and his family lived. The Parks family sold their furniture and, as seen on their receipt from Howard Van Lines, took little with them to start a new life in Michigan.

FORM **1040**
U.S. Treasury Department
Internal Revenue Service

U. S. INDIVIDUAL INCOME TAX RETURN—1959

or Other Taxable Year Beginning _Jan 1_ 1959, Ending _Jan 1_, 19_60_
(PLEASE TYPE OR PRINT)

Name _Raymond A + Rosa L. Parks_
(If this is a joint return of husband and wife, use first names and middle initials of both)

Home address _1930 W. Grand Blvd_
(Number and street or rural route)

Detroit   _8_   _Mich_
(City, town, or post office)   (Postal zone number)   (State)

Your Social Security Number | Occupation _Barber_ | Wife's Social Security Number | Occupation _Seamstress_

ATTACH CHECK OR MONEY ORDER HERE

Exemptions

1. Check blocks which apply. Check for wife only if all of her income is included in this return, or if she had no income.
   - (a) Regular $600 exemption .... ☑ Yourself ☑ Wife | Enter number of exemptions checked
   - (b) Additional $600 exemption if 65 or over at end of taxable year. ☐ Yourself ☐ Wife
   - (c) Additional $600 exemption if blind at end of taxable year..... ☐ Yourself ☐ Wife

   → 2

2. List first names of your children who qualify as dependents; give address if different from yours; _____ | Enter number of children listed →

3. Enter number of exemptions claimed for other persons listed at top of page 2 ....

4. Enter the total number of exemptions claimed on lines 1, 2, and 3 .... → 2

Income

5. Enter all wages, salaries, bonuses, commissions, tips, and other compensation before payroll deductions (including any excess of expense account or similar allowance paid by your employer over your ordinary and necessary business expenses. See instructions, pp. 5-6.)

Employer's Name	Where Employed (City and State)	(a) Wages, etc.	(b) Income Tax Withheld
Michigan Barber School, Inc.		$ _191.70_	$ _6.60_
Harvey's Barber Shop		_219.36_	
Sewing (W)		_250_	
	Enter totals here →	$ _661.06_	$ _6.60_

6. Less: Excludable "Sick Pay" in line 5 (See instructions, page 7. Attach required statement.) ... | $ |
7. Balance (line 5 less line 6). .... | $ |

If the social security tax (FICA) withheld from wages exceeded $120 because you or your wife had more than one employer, see instructions, page 5.

8. Profit (or loss) from business from separate Schedule C............. ♦ | $ |
9. Profit (or loss) from farming from separate Schedule F............ ♦ | $ |
10. Other income (or loss) from page 3 (Dividends, Interest, Rents, Pensions, etc.). ♦ | $ |
11. Adjusted Gross Income (sum of lines 7, 8, 9, and 10) .... | $ _661.06_ |

● Check if unmarried "Head of Household" ☐, or "Surviving Widow or Widower" with dependent child ☐. (See instructions pp. 7-8)

Tax due or refund

12. TAX on income on line 11. (If line 11 is under $5,000, and you do not itemize deductions, use Tax Table on page 16 of instructions to find your tax and check here ☑. If line 11 is $5,000 or more, or if you itemize deductions, compute your tax on page 2 and enter here the amount from line 9, page 2). $ _none_

If income was all from wages, omit lines 13 through 16
13. (a) Dividends received credit from line 5 of Schedule J..... $
    (b) Retirement income credit from line 12 of Schedule K.... $
14. Balance (line 12 less line 13)............... $
15. Enter your self-employment tax from separate Schedule C or F..... $
16. Sum of lines 14 and 15............... $ _none_

17. (a) Tax withheld (line 5 above). Attach Forms W-2, Copy B......... $ _6.60_
    (b) Payments and credits on 1959 Declaration of Estimated Tax (See page 8, instructions.) ● $
    District Director's office where paid _____

18. If your tax (line 12 or 16) is larger than your payments (line 17), enter the **BALANCE DUE** here → $
    Pay in full with this return to "Internal Revenue Service." If less than $1.00, file return without payment.

19. If your payments (line 17) are larger than your tax (line 12 or 16), enter the **OVERPAYMENT** here → $ _6.60_
    If less than $1.00, the overpayment will be refunded only upon application.

20. Amount of line 19 to be: (a) Credited on 1960 estimated tax $_____; (b) Refunded $ _6.60_

Did you receive an expense allowance or reimbursement, or charge expenses to your employer?. ☐ Yes ☑ No See page 6, instructions.
If "Yes," did you submit an itemized accounting of expenses to your employer? .... ☐ Yes ☐ No

County in which you live. _Wayne_	Is your wife (husband) filing a separate return for 1959? ☐ Yes ☑ No. If "yes," enter her (his) name and do not claim the exemption on this return.	If you owe any Federal tax for years before 1959, enter here the Internal Revenue District where the account is outstanding.

I declare under the penalties of perjury that this return (including any accompanying schedules and statements) has been examined by me and to the best of my knowledge and belief is a true, correct, and complete return. If the return is prepared by a person other than the taxpayer, his declaration is based on all the information relating to the matters required to be reported in the return of which he has any knowledge.

Sign here _____
(Taxpayer's signature and date)   (If this is a joint return, BOTH HUSBAND AND WIFE MUST SIGN)   (Wife's signature and date)

_____
(Signature of preparer other than taxpayer)   (Address)   (Date)
o70--16--75313-1

In 1955, Rosa and Raymond Parks had a combined income of more than $3,700. During the bus boycott, when Parks spoke nationwide on behalf of the NAACP and the Montgomery Improvement Association, she received no pay for her services. As the couple's 1959 federal tax return shows, their income plummeted following the boycott and her departure from Hampton.

THE TROUBLES OF BUS BOYCOTT'S FORGOTTEN WOMAN

MONTGOMERY, ALA., HEROINE

By ALEX POINSETT

Fingerprinted in Montgomery, Mrs. Parks was fined $14.

Off in the kitchen corner of a two-room, Detroit apartment last week, hung a dish cloth—limp, ragged, but clean. At a nearby stove toiled a nervous bespectacled little woman—gaunt but cheerful. Like the dish cloth she had once been a faithful servant whose refusal to yield her seat to a white man back in 1955 touched off a year-long boycott that wiped out Montgomery, Ala., bus segregation.

But dish cloths are sometimes lost and forgotten in the whirlpool of history. And so Rosa Louise Parks is today just a tattered rag of her former self—penniless, debt-ridden, ailing with stomach ulcers and a throat tumor, compressed into two rooms with her husband and mother.

The tumor has affected her speech but not her spirit. "If I had it to do all over again," said Mrs. Parks while eating her breakfast: "I would still do it even though I know what I know now."

Shuffling through yellowed newspaper stories of her past exploits as if sorting her memories, the 47-year-old seamstress recalled how she had helped raise thousands of dollars for churches and the NAACP at scores of fundraising rallies around the country, how the extensive traveling from 1956 to 1959 had not been "as glamorous as it seems," how none of the rallies netted her more than $100 beyond expenses.

12

NOW ILL, POVERTY-STRICKEN

Persuaded by a Detroit brother to join him in August 1957 after she lost her $30-a-week assistantship to a department store tailor (Mr. Parks only earned $40-a-week as a barber), the boycott heroine worked in 1958 at Hampton (Va.) Institute, supervising its guest rooms. And although the position earned her $3,600 a year, she was forced to quit because she was unable to move her ailing mother and husband from Detroit.

Nor did times get better for Mrs. Parks after returning to her family. Detroit's high cost of living soon wiped out her $1,300 savings. Her husband, Raymond, 57, hospitalized in July 1958 with pneumonia, was jobless from January to August 1959 and ineligible for unemployment compensation. By October she was obliged to give up a $70-a-month apartment "to reduce expenses." Mrs. Parks accepted two small rooms at Detroit's Progressive Civic League meeting hall, agreed to pay $40 a month with the understanding that her husband was to be a caretaker.

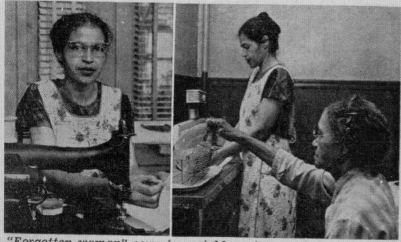

"Forgotten woman" sews for neighbors to earn "extra change," shares two rooms and use of kitchen with mother, husband.

13

"[We] surprised the world and ourselves at the success of the protest," wrote Parks in the wake of the boycott and the Supreme Court ruling. "Our non-violent protest has proven to all that no intelligent, right-thinking person is satisfied with less than human rights that are enjoyed by all people." She gave a great deal of thought to what was necessary for the civil rights movement to continue, jotting down her thoughts on the next steps:

> Much to be done in pooling our resources to gain economic freedom—getting the ballot and using it wisely to gain political freedom. We need to take a critical, honest look at ourselves in regards to the contribution we are making in this period of transition as we approach this new day of freedom. We should be more aware of our own mistakes and try to correct them before being too critical of others.
>
> Our needs: Faith in God. In Him is our strength and courage, our being. Firm convictions of manhood and womanhood and courage to stand by them. Belief in the integrity of our fellow man. Christian love for all God's children. Help plan for a better world of tomorrow by giving all the love, care and guidance to our children of today.

In the early 1960s, young activists took the lead in major challenges to segregation with the Freedom Rides and lunch-counter sit-ins. Parks continued attending NAACP meetings and was present for two seminal events, the March on Washington in 1963 and the March from Selma to Montgomery in 1965. Landmark legislation followed both marches, delineating the high point of the movement—the Civil Rights Act of 1964, which outlawed employment discrimination, and the Voting Rights Act of 1965, which guaranteed all citizens the right to vote. That year, on the tenth anniversary of her arrest on the bus, Parks told the press, "I'd do it again," despite the personal hardships it caused her. "There is a very hard core resistance," she said of those who continued to oppose racial equality. "But, if we do everything we can to spread good will, perhaps someday it will collapse." Although she continued to appear at events, her life had settled down. Working as a receptionist for Congressman Conyers of Michigan's First District brought her a very modest but reliable income, and the lawmaker could not have asked for a more informed staff member than Parks to serve on his social services committee.

The racial violence that broke out later in the 1960s was particularly upsetting to Parks, especially in the summer of 1967, when Detroit was engulfed in four days of rioting following a police raid on an illegal bar. More than forty people were killed, hundreds were arrested and injured, and there was more than $40 million in property damage. Knowing the causes of unrest, Parks remarked, "If you looked beneath the surface, we could see the frustration of some of these people . . . the deprivation." On the other, much larger hand, it was especially vexing to her that some considered the rioting and thievery a form of protest "in the name of civil rights." The burning and looting just a block from her home horrified Parks, who described the destruction in more personal terms as "a very, very severe blow to my husband." Raymond's barbershop was ransacked, and because the Parkses knew some of the looters, it was all the more devastating. "These people had given him quite a bit of work, and had been his customers," said Parks. "It was such a severe thing to him that he couldn't eat or sleep. . . . It was hard on all of us."

The assassination of her old friend Martin Luther King Jr. the following April left Parks grief stricken but not surprised, given the bloodshed that had always surrounded the movement—ironically a movement that preached nonviolence. Picking up where King had left off, Parks arrived in Memphis, where he had been meeting with striking garbage collectors, and met with some of the men herself. Her next stop was Atlanta for the funeral.

Years before, in what could have been his epitaph, she wrote on the back of an envelope her admiration for "his devout Christianity, genial manner, quiet militancy, and his power of persuasion," all of which combined to make him "a true leader."

Bloodied seminarian John Lewis and college student James Zwerg, who was beaten unconscious at a bus station in Montgomery by whites furious at the arrival of the Freedom Riders, wait for an ambulance, May 20, 1961. In her eighties, Parks would regularly accompany students on her Pathways to Freedom summer bus trips that traced the routes of the Freedom Rides and stopped at historic sites.

This aerial view shows thousands of people walking from Selma to Montgomery in March 1965. The march followed a voter registration campaign marked by mass arrests and police brutality and coincided with the introduction of a bill in Congress to expand voting rights. Marchers demanded federal protection for the newly registered voters to ensure their safety at the polls. On the last day of the fifty-four-mile, five-day trek, Parks joined in and was later escorted to the front of the march at Montgomery's Court Square. (It was there eight years before that she had boarded the bus that would drive her into American history.)

From Court Square, Rosa Parks, Ralph Abernathy, Juanita Abernathy, Ralph Bunche, Martin Luther King Jr., and Coretta Scott King led some twenty-five thousand marchers to the Alabama state capitol. By popular demand, Parks delivered some impromptu remarks to the crowd. In August, President Lyndon B. Johnson signed the 1965 Voting Rights Act into law.

Parks introduced New York representative Shirley Chisholm, the first black woman elected to Congress, when the newly installed lawmaker gave an address at a Women's Public Affairs Committee (WPAC) meeting in Detroit in 1969. Three years later Parks campaigned for Senator George McGovern for president, but she also supported Chisholm's "Unbossed and Unbought" long-shot candidacy. Although Parks did not regard herself as part of the growing feminist movement, her involvement in WPAC grew out of her disappointment with how women in civil rights work were often treated by male colleagues.

In her sixties, Rosa Parks was still at work—both for Congressman Conyers and for her fellow citizens—when others were settling into retirement. In 1974, drawing on her painful experience from thirty years earlier in assisting rape victims and as a continuance of her civil rights activities, she cofounded yet another group, the Free Joan Little Defense Committee of Detroit. Little, imprisoned in North Carolina, was the first woman charged with committing murder during a sexual assault to successfully claim self-defense. Even as Parks aged and slowed down, she found it difficult not to act when she saw someone in need or to say no when someone asked for help. "I don't feel like I really have a private life," she said at the time. "There are many other things that need my attention."

Parks was sixty-four years old when both her husband and brother died in 1977; her mother followed two years later. These three had meant the most to her, and her own health suffered as she developed a heart ailment. But her friendship with Elaine Steele, a young woman with whom she had briefly worked as a seamstress, was a vital, welcome salve in surviving such a trying period. Steele helped manage her affairs, as Parks remained frequently in demand as a speaker or honorary chairman. Pacing herself later in life, Parks finally started taking occasional vacations, visiting with family and friends on the West Coast. Her long-held dream, though, was to found something other than aid committees and defense funds but rather to establish a means to educate and motivate young people.

In 1987, Parks and Steele founded the Rosa and Raymond Parks Institute for Self Development. "We work with young people, from the ages of 11 to 17, and our main program is the Pathways to Freedom," Parks explained. Activities included job training, leadership development, and conflict resolution. The institute also became known for its summer bus trips, with Parks along for the ride from the Deep South to Canada. The tours followed routes on the Underground Railroad and interstate highways where the Freedom Riders once rode against segregation on buses. "We hope that will inspire and give them a sense of history," Parks said when the program began. She always encouraged young people "to have a spiritual awareness because I feel that with the spirit within and our belief in ourselves and our faith in God that we will overcome many obstacles that we could not with negative attitudes. I want to always think

Parks's skills as a seamstress extended to creating her own dresses. Here, a model walks the runway at a New York City fashion show wearing a dress Parks designed, October 17, 1975.

in terms of being positive, and them being positive, and believing in themselves, and believing that they should be good citizens and an asset to our country."

During her last decade and a half, Parks wrote an autobiography, *My Story* (1992), and two other inspirational works and continued to speak out. In 1991, she issued a lengthy statement opposing the nomination of Judge Clarence Thomas, an African American, to the U.S. Supreme Court. Parks cited "his statements on the *Brown v. Board of Education* case, on affirmative action, and even on . . . *Roe v. Wade*" as indications that "he wants to push [the] clock back. African Americans, I believe, want to have confidence in the promise of the courts, we want to believe that they are a place we can turn for the redress of the racial discrimination and many deprivations that are still clearly rampant in our country."

Parks was at the center of worldwide attention and outrage in 1994 after a young thief, who recognized her,

robbed and beat her in her own home. "I tried to defend myself and grabbed his shirt. Even at eighty-one years of age, I felt it was my right to defend myself," she said. The attack and her sympathetic response to his plight as a "sick-minded" person prompted reams of editorials and public soul-searching. With the help of various contributors, anonymous or unsung, she spent her last years in a safe high-rise apartment with an idyllic view of the Detroit River. At the close of the twentieth century, the span of which closely paralleled Parks's lifetime, her contributions to the civil rights movement and her calls for justice received renewed attention. Her last years coincided with major civil rights anniversaries, and in the 1990s she received numerous honors. "It's nice to be remembered," she would say in response.

On October 24, 2005, five weeks before the fiftieth anniversary of her bus protest, Parks died in her Detroit home. Funeral memorials occurred across the country. She lay in repose at St. Paul's AME Church in Montgomery, where fellow Alabaman and Secretary of State Condoleezza Rice spoke of Parks's influence on her life. Over the course of two days, some fifty thousand people passed Parks's casket in the rotunda of the U.S. Capitol in Washington, D.C., where she lay in honor, the first woman granted such a tribute. During a seven-hour Victory Celebration of Life, the Greater Grace Temple Church in Detroit was filled to its four-thousand-seat capacity with family, friends, former U.S. presidents, members of Congress, and more than a hundred honorary pallbearers. She was buried between her mother and husband in the Rosa L. Parks Freedom Chapel at Woodlawn Cemetery in Detroit.

Long plagued with stress-related health issues,
Parks took up yoga and became a vegetarian in the 1970s.
Here she demonstrates the bow pose.

Kwame Ture (formerly Stokely Carmichael), a leader in the Black Power movement, and Parks at the University of Michigan, Ann Arbor, following a forum on civil rights in February 1983. This copy of the widely published photograph belonged to Parks.

5.

Visa denials to Cubans to come to the U.S. to talk with us.
Press is uniform in response to travel to Cuba. Challenge of all of us to Counteract the War w/Cuba

— — ~ — — — — —

Racial diser in Cuba darker – lighter nothing like U.S. different quality U.S brought segregation to Cuba.

During the 1980s, amid frequent reports of atrocities in Latin America, Parks attended lectures on the policies, covert activities, and involvement of the United States in Central America and the Caribbean. She saved more than twenty pages of notes, including this page, which would have been especially relevant to her, with its mention that the "U.S. brought segregation to Cuba."

On African American Quilt Discovery Day at the Detroit Historical Museum in 1986, Parks posed with an appliqued floral medallion quilt that she completed in 1949. It was later registered with the Michigan Quilt Project Collection at Michigan State University.

A pious member of the African Methodist Episcopal church since childhood, Parks began attending St. Matthew's in Detroit, contributing regularly on her modest salary and becoming a deaconess in 1965. In that role, she helped produce the church bulletin, visited shut-ins, served meals, and greeted visitors.

This Michigan driver's license reflects how things had changed for Parks, who had once relied almost exclusively on public transportation. A colleague in Congressman Conyers's office referred to her large choice of vehicle as "a tank." Driving her own car, she turned up everywhere—at rallies, labor strikes, demonstrations, teach-ins, wherever she felt she could offer support.

FEBRUARY 1989

Monday	Tuesday	Wednesday

JANUARY

S	M	T	W	T	F	S
1	2	3	4	5	6	7
8	9	10	11	12	13	14
15	16	17	18	19	20	21
22	23	24	25	26	27	28
29	30	31				

MARCH

S	M	T	W	T	F	S
			1	2	3	4
5	6	7	8	9	10	11
12	13	14	15	16	17	18
19	20	21	22	23	24	25
26	27	28	29	30	31	

1

6 Univ. of Wis.
"How has Amer.
Changed? Where
do you see it
going."
Laurie Hildebrandt
$5,000
608·262·2684

7 Wash. D.C.
Brian Lankard

8 (US) Wash. DC
Brian Lankard

13 Miss
Walker

14 (US)

15

20 (US)
L.A.

21
L.A.

22
Leave for
Las Vegas

27
Illinois State
Univ.
$3,500
Chiba X Namari
309· 438-8611
309· 438-3868

28

US-United States, C-Canada, UK-United Kingdom, J-Japan

Having marked Saturday, February 4, as "My 76th birthday" in her 1989 calendar, Parks filled the rest of the dates with a busy speaking schedule that took her to the University of Wisconsin; Washington, D.C.; Chattanooga; Jackson State University; Pasadena and Los Angeles; Las Vegas; St. Louis; and Illinois State University. Her activities in the 1980s included supporting Jesse Jackson's presidential campaigns, working for the designation of a federal holiday in honor of Martin Luther King Jr., chairing Meals on Wheels holiday drives, and continuing to establish prisoner defense funds.

Thursday	Friday	May de 76 Sat/Sun
2 D.C. Tribute?	3	4 Birthday
		5
9 Tenn.	10 Tenn. Martin Marietta Energy Systems $5,000 Gail L. Swell 615·574·9218	11 (J) Jackson, Miss. Margaret Walker
		12 Jackson, Miss. Walker
16 Jackson State Univ. $3,500 Miss.	17 Pasadena, Ca.? $3,000	18 Blk Woman's Forum Luncheon Opra Winfrey M.C. L.A, Ca $10,000 19 L.A.
23 Las Vegas $3,500 Joan Burkhart 702·383·0268	24 Leave for St Louis	25 Henry Brown $3,500 26

Parks and her friend Elaine Steele meet with
children taking part in the Rosa and Raymond
Parks Institute's Pathways to Freedom School
and Tri-State Day Camp, ca. 1990.

Parks met with Pope John Paul II following a prayer
service at the Cathedral Basilica in St. Louis, January
27, 1999. She presented the pontiff with a copy of
her book *Quiet Strength* (1994), a collection of her
contemplations and short essays.

Parks and Jane Gunter, the passenger who had offered her
bus seat to Parks, were reunited thirty-seven years after
that historic bus ride in Montgomery. Meeting in 1992 in
downtown Atlanta, the two compared their memories
of that day. "You were there," Parks confirmed. Each had
just published a book, and each signed copies for the
other. Parks, so active in her own church, was delighted
to learn that Gunter worked as a missionary, becoming a
pastor and founder of Family Life Ministries. Later, Gunter
regularly teamed up with Elaine Steele, cofounder of the
Parks Institute, to give civil rights talks to students.

In Michigan, Parks joined President Clinton, second from right, on the campaign trail during his 1996 run for reelection. Also standing on stage are Senator Carl Levin of Michigan, far left, Congressman Dale Kildee, Pontiac mayor Walter Moore, and Elaine Steele, to the left of Parks.

Parks, center, in gray, deftly brandishes a shovel during the groundbreaking ceremonies for the Rosa Parks Museum and Library at Troy University, Montgomery, in 1998. Johnnie Carr, a civil rights activist and a friend since the 1920s, and Elaine Steele, director of the Parks Institute, are to the left of her.

> *Funeral* My funeral expenses have been paid by me to the Swanson Funeral Home, 806 East Grand Boulevard, grave site, Woodlawn Cemetery, Detroit, Michigan. I request a brief funeral program at the St. Matthew A.M.E. Church where I am a member. No long speeches. Instead of flowers, donations may be made to the Youth Education Dept/ Missionary of St. Matthew Church, and the R + R Parks Institute.

Having sat through many lectures, sermons, and talks in her lifetime, Parks asked that mourners at her funeral not be subjected to "long speeches." These notes are from a handwritten document she titled "Living Will and Testament of R.L.P."

Rosa Parks became the first woman and the second African American to lie in honor in the rotunda of the U.S. Capitol. Following her death on October 24, 2005, the Senate approved this rare distinction, and on October 30–31 thousands who waited in long lines paid their respects. President George W. Bush and First Lady Laura Bush attended her memorial service.

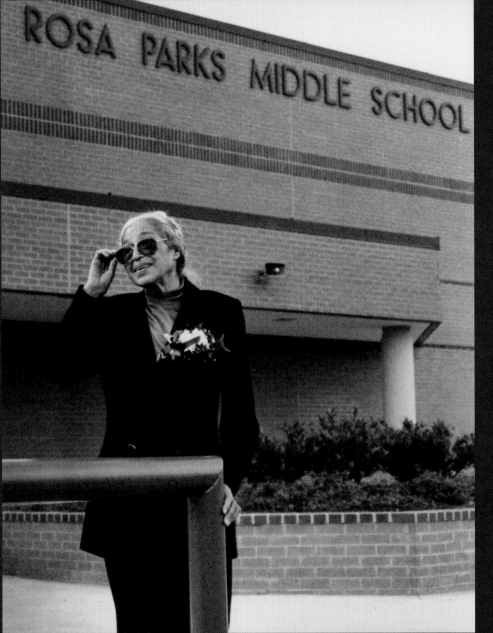

Parks dedicated a new
middle school named
in her honor in Olney,
Maryland, on April 29,
1993. Eighty years old
at the time, she told
the crowd she would
continue working for
"peace and justice"
as long as she could.

CHAPTER 4 Legacy

In the 1950s, Rosa Parks was called "that woman who caused all the trouble"—and far worse—yet those who actually knew her almost invariably described her as gentle. If no one ever witnessed her fury, perhaps it was because she chose to write about it instead. Eventually, "that agitator" from Montgomery was regarded as a living cultural icon and an American patriot. The NAACP investigator who looked into cases no one wanted to hear about became the public speaker everyone wanted to hear from. The citizen who was twice turned away from registering to vote was invited to the White House. The seamstress who lost her low-paying department store job was given a bronze statue in the U.S. Capitol. The bus passenger who was arrested and put in a police car had a museum and library named for her at that very spot. And the woman who struggled with poverty and financial insecurity left an archive valued in the millions and a legacy that was invaluable.

As early as the 1960s, Parks was called the mother of the civil rights movement. If her only influence was to galvanize the fight for racial justice, that would have been more than enough. But she was more interested in what the movement produced, and she worked diligently for tangible results by educating voters, supporting activists, and campaigning for political candidates committed to positive change. What gave her the greatest pride were the achievements that followed, "the fact that we have acquired enough freedom . . . to be vocal and to say what we wish, act as human beings, and . . . to see many of our people in top positions in the government, all the way from Washington to local government."

Toward the end of her life, governments, universities, and organizations—even those that had once operated as Montgomery

I want to be remembered as a person who wanted to be free and wanted others to be free.

had—bestowed their highest honors on her with words of lofty praise. Her own words were decidedly more humble. "I would like to be remembered as one who has always cared for people," she said simply. "I have more concern for people than material things. I have always wanted to help people—people in need, who are ill, in trouble or need help financially. I have always been very sympathetic for those people who need someone to care."

In an Oval Office ceremony at the White House, President Bill Clinton awarded Parks the Presidential Medal of Freedom, September 9, 1996.

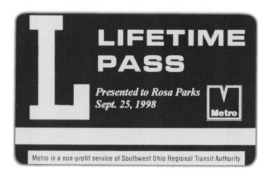

Among the forms of recognition Parks received for her civil rights work, a simple but especially symbolic one was a Lifetime Pass issued to her by the Southwest Ohio Regional Transit Authority on September 25, 1998.

Parks received an honorary doctorate in humane letters from Mount St. Vincent University, Nova Scotia, 1998.

On June 16, 1999, in the rotunda of the U.S. Capitol before a thousand spectators, Parks received the Congressional Gold Medal, the highest civilian award granted by Congress. One of those in attendance—and seated in the front row, no less—was Senator Strom Thurmond (R-S.C.), who, after the Montgomery Bus Boycott, had filibustered for twenty-four hours, eighteen minutes on the Senate floor in opposition to the Civil Rights Act of 1957. In her brief remarks, Parks observed, "This medal is encouragement for all of us to continue until all have rights." In 2005, at the Victory Celebration of Life memorial service for Parks at Detroit's Greater Grace Temple Church, House Minority Leader Nancy Pelosi (D-Calif.) said of her being a Gold Medal recipient, "It brought honor to Rosa but it added luster to the award. Everyone who received it since then and in the future will have an award that is more important because Rosa Parks has received it."

Twelfth Street, a major thoroughfare in Detroit, was renamed Rosa Parks Boulevard in 1976. Here, Parks poses with a news reporter, left, and friends Louise Tappes and Mary Sims, along with some preliminary street signage.

until justice rolls down
like waters
and righteousness
like a mighty stream

Dr. Martin Luther King, Jr.

Sponsored by the Alpha Kappa Alpha Sorority and the Alabama Historical Association, a historical marker was installed in 2008 at the spot on Dexter Avenue in Montgomery where Rosa Parks boarded the bus on December 1, 1955.

The second casting of Erik Blome's life-size bronze statue (2009) of Parks on a bus seat occupies the central portion of Rosa Parks Plaza at the Dallas Area Rapid Transit West End Station in Dallas, Texas. The original sculpture is on display at the Rosa Parks Museum in Montgomery.

The Struggle, Continues,
We must ~~keeping moving~~
to reach our goal of
~~freedom peace~~

equality,   The
  We must

                The

        The Struggle Continues
The   as we to ~~the~~ ~~for~~ enter
        ~~the~~ 199 0s with love, dedication
            faith and hope toward ~~the~~

        The struggle & continues ~~to~~
        ~~to~~ We must keep alive ~~the~~
        ~~Dr. Martin kings~~ Dr. Kings
            dream of the Beloved Community

                    ~~tothe~~ The Struggle Continu~~es~~
                as we keep alive Kinting's
                Dream of the Beloved
                Com~~m~~

On the back of a pharmacy bag, Parks
sketched her thoughts on the theme
"The Struggle Continues," ca. 1990.
Given the nature of her life's work
and the society she lived in, she could
have written it at almost any time.

Acknowledgments

In writing this book, it was a privilege to share the page with Rosa Parks, whose words on freedom, justice, and equality are just as important now as when she spoke and wrote them.

Many thanks go to the Library of Congress Publishing Office staff: Becky Clark, director, Peter Devereaux, Hannah Freece, Aimee Hess, and Margaret Wagner, and our efficient interns, Tamia Williams and Aia Yousef. All made essential contributions. I also appreciate the helpful insights and suggestions from Library colleagues Carroll Johnson-Welsh, senior exhibit director, and Adrienne Cannon, manuscript specialist, whose work on *Rosa Parks: In Her Own Words*, the exhibition, helped frame the book.

Elaine Steele and Anita Peek, of the Rosa and Raymond Parks Institute for Self-Development, and longtime close friends of Rosa Parks, very kindly furnished their expertise on her life. Jane Gunter graciously shared her experience as a passenger on that historic Montgomery bus, and Brenda Davenport of the Southern Christian Leadership Conference generously offered her recollections of friendship with Parks. Steve Cohen provided valuable assistance in securing images. I offer a hearty thank-you to each of them.

I am very grateful to the University of Georgia Press for its generous interest in this project, and I especially thank Lisa Bayer, Walter Biggins, Jon Davies, and Erin Kirk New for their thoughtful work.

Notes

Quotations from Rosa Parks are cited below. Those from sources in the Rosa Parks Papers (RPP) in the Library of Congress Manuscript Division include an mss number; these items can be located by searching for that number at www.loc.gov.

1   *Is it worthwhile to reveal . . .*   RPP, mss85943.0227 [image 24]

1   *the dark closet of my . . .*   RPP, mss85943.0227 [image 2]

1   *was like walking a tightrope . . .*   RPP, mss85943.0235 [image 9]

1   *determination to go on with . . .*   RPP, mss85943.0225 [image 4]

3   *I stayed awake many nights . . .*   RPP, mss85943.0227 [image 28]

3   *KKK moved through the country . . .*   RPP, mss85943.0227 [image 27]

3   *never had a whole lot . . .*   RPP, mss85943.0230 [image 16]

3   *There were times when we . . .*   RPP, mss85943.0230 [image 16]

4   *Life of extreme poverty because . . .*   RPP, mss85943.0227 [image 26]

4   *events that I could look . . .*   RPP, mss85943.0230 [image 18]

8   *My mother was a very . . .*   RPP, mss85943.0227 [image 28]

9   *I adored my brother and . . .*   RPP, mss85943.0227 [images 28–29]

12   *I would rather be lynched . . .*   RPP, mss85943.0227 [images 3, 5, and 7]

12   *was fast becoming intoxicated on . . .*   RPP, mss85943.0227 [images 12–22]

12   *the requested book will be . . .*   RPP, mss85943.0226 [image 6]

15   *It is not easy to remain . . .*   RPP, mss85943.0226 [image 14]

15   *In our airport in Montgomery . . .*   RPP, mss85943.0226 [image 14]

15   *We soothe ourselves with the . . .*   RPP, mss85943.0226 [image 29]

15   *where segregation was the order . . .*   RPP, mss85943.0225 [image 9]

15   *never to accept it, even . . .*   RPP, mss85943.0225 [image 9]

15   *There was no solution for us . . .*   RPP, mss85943.0225 [image 9]

15   *search for a way of . . .*   RPP, mss85943.0225 [image 9]

17   *The schools in the south*   RPP, mss85943.0226

18   *early childhood*   RPP, mss85943.0227 [image 25]

18   *histories of others—Crispus Attucks . . .*   RPP, mss85943.0225 [image 9]

18   *the police had killed two . . .*   Rosa Parks with Jim Haskins, *Rosa Parks: My Story* (New York: Dial Books, 1992), 69

18   *cases of police brutality, rape . . .*   RPP, mss85943.0225 [image 9]

18   *it was terribly hard getting . . .*   Parks with Haskins, *Rosa Parks: My Story*, 69

18   *I was forty-two years old . . .*   Douglas Brinkley, *Rosa Parks* (New York: Penguin Books, 2000), 95

22   *The whole Scottsboro ordeal was* . . .   Brinkley, *Rosa Parks*, 95

27   *I felt if I did* . . .   RPP, mss85943.0230 [image 11]

29   *If I had been paying* . . .   Parks with Haskins, *Rosa Parks: My Story*, 113

29   *I felt just resigned to* . . .   RPP, mss85943.0230 [image 22]

29   *The atmosphere was very, I* . . .   Interview with Rosa Parks, conducted by Blackside, Inc., on November 14, 1985, for *Eyes on the Prize: America's Civil Rights Years (1954–1965)*, Washington University Libraries, Film and Media Archive, Henry Hampton Collection

33   *Well, we hope to achieve* . . .   Rosa Parks interview, *Manufacturing Intellect*, video, 1995

33   *policemen began arresting drivers—forbidding* . . .   RPP, mss85943.0225 [image 12]

33   *wearing out their cars, bought* . . .   RPP, mss85943.0177 [image 2]

33   *I worked five long, tense* . . .   RPP, mss85943.0226 [image 25]

34   *remember how long some of* . . .   RPP, **mss85943.0177 [image 3]**

37   *put the bus company out* . . .   Rosa Parks interview, *The Merv Griffin Show*, 1983

41   *I am rushing now to* . . .   RPP, mss85943.0013 [image 9]

41   *ride as free men*   RPP, mss85943.0357 [image 2]

41   *Another shipment of shoes came* . . .   RPP, mss85943.0013 [image 2]

41   *I suppose the people there* . . .   RPP, mss85943.0013 [image 12]

41   *Do your best and I* . . .   RPP, mss85943.0013 [image 2]

41   *I am leaving N.Y. now* . . .   RPP, mss85943.0013 [image 14]

41   *Today's Supreme Court decision. Happy* . . .   RPP, mss85943.0225 [image 8]

41   *We didn't sag at all* . . .   Rosa Parks interview, *Eyes on the Prize*, video, 1985

41   *because there were so many* . . .   Rosa Parks interview, *Eyes on the Prize*, video, 1985

47   *The only thing we can* . . .   RPP, mss85943.0022 [image 2]

48   *My social life is practically* . . .   RPP, mss85943.0015 [image 42]

48   *My darling husband, Hearing your* . . .   RPP, mss85943.0021 [image 5]

48   *I wrote the doctor for* . . .   RPP, mss85943.0021 [image 8]

48   *I read the two articles* . . .   RPP, mss85943.0021 [image 9]

48   *The exray of my stomach* . . .   RPP, mss85943.0022 [image 4]

49   *I have to stay on* . . .   RPP, mss85943.0022 [image 6]

49   *My birthday was quite well* . . .   RPP, mss85943.0022 [image 12]

49   *I will go to the* . . .   RPP, mss85943.0015 [image 16]

49   *I was so glad to* . . .   RPP, mss85943.0022 [image 15]

49   *the promised land that wasn't*   Jeanne Theoharis, *The Rebellious Life of Mrs. Rosa Parks* (Boston: Beacon Press, 2013), 167

49   *the bus boycott's forgotten woman*   *Jet*, July 14, 1960, RPP, mss85943.0343 [image 2]

51   *I would never leave you* . . .   RPP, mss85943.0023 [image 9]

56   *surprised the world and ourselves* . . .   RPP, mss85943.0225 [image 18]

56   *Much to be done in* . . .   RPP, mss85943.0225 [images 9–10]

56   *There is a very hard* . . .   "'I'd Do It Again,' Mrs. Parks Says: 'Too Tired' To Give White Man Her Seat, She Sparked Boycott," *Chicago Daily Defender*, daily ed. (1960–1973), January 3, 1966

56   *If you looked beneath the* . . .   RPP, mss85943.0230 [image 25]

56   *a very, very severe blow* . . .   RPP, mss85943.0230 [image 25]

56   *These people had given him* . . .   RPP, mss85943.0230 [image 26]

57   *his devout Christianity, genial manner* . . .   RPP, mss85943.0225 [image 18]

59   *I don't feel like I* . . .   RPP, mss85943.0230 [image 27]

59   *We work with young people,* . . .   Rosa Parks interview, *Manufacturing Intellect*, video, 1995

59   *We hope that will inspire* . . .   Rosa Parks interview, *Manufacturing Intellect*, video, 1995

59   *to have a spiritual awareness* . . .   Rosa Parks interview, *Manufacturing Intellect*, video, 1995

60   *his statements on the* Brown . . .   RPP, mss85943.0237 [image 2]

60   *I tried to defend myself* . . .   Jeanne Theoharis, "1944 Mugging Reveals Rosa Park's True Character," *Women's eNews*, February 2, 2013, womensenews.org

71   *I want to be remembered* . . .   Rosa Parks with Gregory J. Reed, *Quiet Strength* (Grand Rapids: Zondervan Publishing House, 1994), 86

71   *the fact that we have* . . .   RPP, mss85943.0230 [image 28]

72   *I would like to be* . . .   RPP, mss85943.0229 [image 4]

Sources and Suggested Reading

Brinkley, Douglas. *Rosa Parks*. New York: Viking/Penguin, 2003.

McGuire, Danielle. *At the Dark End of the Street*. New York: Alfred A. Knopf, 2010.

Parks, Rosa, with Jim Haskins. *My Story*. New York: Dial Books, 1992.

Parks, Rosa, with Gregory J. Reed. *Quiet Strength*. Grand Rapids: Zondervan Publishing, 1994.

Theoharis, Jeanne. *The Rebellious Life of Mrs. Rosa Parks*. Boston: Beacon Press, 2013.

Library of Congress Resources

The Rosa Parks Collection, Manuscript Division, Library of Congress: https://www.loc.gov/collections/rosa-parks-papers /about-this-collection/

Articles and essays from the Library of Congress: https://www.loc .gov/collections/rosa-parks-papers/articles-and-essays/

In Her Own Words online exhibition: http://www.loc.gov /exhibitions/rosa-parks-in-her-own-words/ about-this-exhibition/.

Image Credits

All images are from the Library of Congress Manuscript Division (MS) or Prints and Photographs Division (P&P) and include an identification number; these items can be located by searching for that number at www.loc.gov. Those from the Rosa Park Papers are abbreviated RPP. Those from the Farm Security Administration / Office of War Information Collection are abbreviated FSA, and those from the New York World Telegram and Sun Collection are abbreviated NYWTS. Rosa Parks's name and image are used with permission from the Rosa and Raymond Parks Institute for Self-Development; these images are noted with the abbreviation (RRPISD). For page numbers, L = left, R = right, T = top, B = bottom.

ii	J. Maschhoff, RRPISD, RPP, P&P, 2015645721
vi	RRPISD, RPP, P&P, 2015647361
2	RRPISD, RPP, P&P, 2015647353
4	RPP, P&P, 2015651329 [image 2]
5	RRPISD, RPP, MS, mss85943.001811 [image 27]
6–7	RPP, MS, mss85943.0498
8L	RPP, P&P, 2015645715
8R	RPP, P&P, 2015645709
9L	RRPISD, RPP, P&P, 2015645701
9R	RPP, P&P, 2015645719
10L	RPP, P&P, 2015645718
10R	RPP, P&P, mss85943.0034
11	RPP, P&P, 2015645717
13	RRPISD, RPP, MS, mss85943.001811 [image 16]
14	Marion Post Walcott, FSA, P&P, 2017753632
15	© Danny Lyon / Magnum Photos, P&P, 00650612
16T	Marion Post Walcott, FSA, P&P, 2017753638
16B	RRPISD, RPP, MS, mss85943.001902 [image 9]
17	Marion Post Walcott, FSA, P&P, 2017753660
19	RRPISD, RPP, P&P, 2015652115
20	RPP, MS, mss85943.001414 [image 2]
21	Esther Bubley, FSA, P&P, 2017862188
22T	RRPISD, RPP, P&P, 2015645702
22B	NYWTS, P&P, 94509133
23T	RPP, MS, mss85943.0323
23B	RPP, MS, mss85943.0422
24–25	RRPISD, RPP, MS, mss85943.001815 [image 34]
26	RRPISD, RPP, MS, mss85943.0239

Index

Featherlite pancakes

sift together
1 C flour

2 T. B. Powder

½ t salt

2 T sugar

mix

1 egg - 1¼ C milk

⅓ C peanut butter
melted
1 T shorting or oil

combine with dry ingredients

Cook at 275°

on griddle

Parks's signature "featherlite pancakes" recipe, jotted on the back of a manila envelope, included a key ingredient: one-third cup of melted peanut butter.